Assel
WALKING-IN-YOUR-SHOES
Walking is Understanding

Christian Assel

WALKING IN YOUR SHOES

WALKING IS UNDERSTANDING

Foreword by actor and filmmaker Joseph Culp

**A Successful Alternative
to Family Constellation Work**

Translated by Jonathan Bruton

LOTUS PRESS

Important Note

The information presented in this book has been carefully researched and passed on to our best knowledge and conscience. Despite this fact, neither the author nor the publisher assume any type of liability for presumed or actual damages of any kind that might result from the direct or indirect application or use of the statements in this book.

The information in this book is solely intended for interested readers and educational purposes and should in no way be understood as diagnostic or therapeutic instructions in the medical sense. If you suspect the existence of an illness, we definitely recommend that you see a physician or healing practitioner and expressly discourage you from diagnosing and treating yourself.

First English Edition 2012
© Lotus Press
Box 325, Twin Lakes, WI 53181, USA
www.lotuspress.com
lotuspress@lotuspress.com
The Shangri-La series is published in cooperation with Windpferd Verlagsgesellschaft mbH, Oberstdorf, Germany
© 2010 by Windpferd Verlagsgesellschaft mbH, Oberstdorf, Germany
All rights reserved
Translated by Jonathan Bruton
Cover design: Kuhn Grafik Communication Design, Amden, Switzerland
Cover image: Thinkstock
Layout and graphic design: Marx Grafik und ArtWork, Germany
ISBN 978-0-9409-8503-2
Library of Congress Control Number: 2012946409
Printed in USA

Table of Contents

Foreword by Joseph Culp

Walking-In-Your-Shoes is a transformational process. It is a method which uses our natural gifts for transcendence and empathy to deeply relate to another being. I often refer to it as "spontaneous empathy." The technique is simple yet profound: In a supportive group setting, or with a facilitator, one states the intention to be another person and begins to move in the space, refraining from imitations or cognitive guesswork, and tunes into the energies and feelings of the body. During the Walking, one experiences a shift of awareness and spontaneously manifests behavior aspects, emotional/psychological states and life-themes of the person they are Walking. The information manifested has been found to have a high degree of accuracy whether the Walker has knowledge of the person or not. People who have been Walked frequently report that they have never before felt so understood and accepted, and those who Walk experience a sense of liberation by temporarily "stepping out" of their often limiting self-concept. The profound implications of this process took me on a personal journey of practice and discovery for over twenty years. I have seen many lives transformed in positive ways by Walking-In-Your-Shoes. Here, at last, in Christian Assel's book, the beauty and wisdom of this process is available for all.

When psychologist Dr. John Cogswell and I first began our investigations into this body/mind technique back in the mid-1980's, we soon discovered that no amount of discussion could adequately explain what was taking place. Cogswell first called it "Walking-In-Your-Shoes" because of the old Native American proverb, "You can never know another human being until you have Walked a mile in his moccasins." We were taking this idea to an experiential level using simple body/mind awareness and we were astonished at the results. How could one simply set an intention and "Walk" as someone else, and spontaneously reveal the other's inner life with such accuracy? To explain the phenomenon is speculative at best and as of today there are no scientific studies that can prove what is happening in this process. We also found great resistance to the practice, in ourselves and others, because the activity of Walking as another challenges some very basic beliefs about the nature of reality. This resistance, we later agreed, is what can make it difficult for a practice like WIYS to flourish. What Cogswell and I and many other therapists, actors, artists, and lay people who helped develop the process could agree on were the beneficial effects of the practice: People were helping other people transform their consciousness through a kind of affective attunement and mirroring, and both the Walker and the person being Walked felt more alive, compassionate and empowered to be their true selves. We saw breakthrough after breakthrough—we could Walk our mothers and fathers, our spouses and partners, our friends and employers, and the ancestors who are still influencing us today. For two decades Cogswell and other therapists continued to explore the technique in the field of psychology, business, conflict resolution and community renewal while I pushed ahead with groups of performing artists. I found in addition to the objectives of the therapeutic model that Walking could be applied to anything one wanted to experience—loved ones, friends, enemies, ancestors, (alive or dead), fictional characters, archetypes, dreams, future planning and ideas. I now consider Walking a foundational tool for the actor, writer and director because it allows both personal and collective unconscious material to naturally manifest through the artist and inform the work at hand, giving it personal connection and deeper resonance. How it works is something for continued research and study, and, as we found, requires some extensive discussions on metaphysical theory. But all intellectual discussion aside, after seeing, guiding and performing hundreds of Walks, the one thing I can be sure of is that the Walking process most certainly does work. It helps people access their gift for "spontaneous empathy," brings about compassion and self-empowerment, and has the potential to transform human lives for the better.

In addition to helping us heal personal wounds, raise self-esteem, facilitate communication in family and society, we need a practice like Walking-In-Your-Shoes to challenge our epistemological view. At the heart of the process is the opportunity for us to break out of our limiting self-concepts and move into our deeper natures of love, compassion and what the Buddhists call "mirror-like wisdom." It's about getting past our rigid concepts about reality and more importantly, about ourselves. It's about letting go, at least temporarily, of the belief we all carry that we are somehow inherently separate. Quantum physics and all the highest teachings in every religion say the same thing: Separateness is an illusion. We are all actually one and we are everything that is. It doesn't matter what you believe. It goes beyond the ego that has to believe in things. It's not about being "psychic" and if it is, then it's the psychic ability in all of us. Of course we can be each other … because we already are.

And now the news is out! Christian Assel's book on Walking-In-Your-Shoes marks a culmination of years of study and practice by many people in this powerful technique. Assel's years of experience in Family Constellation work provides the perfect foundation for WIYS to flourish and grow and find its place in our world. This important book also marks what I hope is a new beginning in modern psychology and contemporary culture, where the use of transpersonal methods become practical and even commonplace. I envision a world where Walking Groups are as common as 12 Step support, yoga class or the gym, but instead where people can go to practice their innate gift for empathy, resolve internal and external conflicts and help empower each other to be more fully alive. Christian Assel's book is the first "step" in a long "Walk" we can take together in transforming our world through this kind of service. I hope it will inspire those looking for an experience of greater depth and aliveness. I hope it will inspire others to practice the technique and form their own Walking groups all over the world. Maybe it will inspire you to take a journey, as I did, to learn that the whole body is the mind and that by simply setting an intention and giving in to emptiness, one can experience other people, other worlds and the deep reaches of the human psyche.

Joseph Culp
August, 2010
Santa Monica, California

Preface

Some years ago in California I followed a "chance" lead and got to know the method known as "Walking-In-Your-Shoes," which at that time was completely unknown in Europe. My teacher was Joseph Culp, co-founder of the technique along with psychotherapist John Cogswell, and my use of it in Germany has ever since resonated strongly with people who have tried it out. This method was developed in the film and theater world. In this context it was initially mainly used to enable actors to achieve a greater depth of emotional resonance with their roles. This allowed actors to become incredibly intimate with the parts they were to play, to identify astonishingly closely with them. It soon became clear, however, that it was also possible to "Walk" roles from real life—for example, real people—an insight which transcended the existing limits of the theatrical. This led to the development of Walking-In-Your-Shoes as we know it today.

The Walking becomes a general tool for learning. It sets things in motion, showing you how you can develop your relationship with a particular person. But an even more crucial element is also involved which is neatly and accurately formulated in the native American proverb: "You can't understand another human being until you walked a mile in his moccasins." The "Walker" steps mentally and emotionally into the shoes—as it were, into the skin—of the person whom he is "Walking." What arises is an expression of inner empathy which manifests in the physical motion of the conscious act of Walking.

In this book I describe many concrete examples from actual practice. I have chosen this approach because my training workshops have shown me that the best way to communicate the method is to rely as far as possible on practical experience and to use only as much theory as you actually need. You do of course need theory to tell your head what to do. Its vital role is to organize the inner and outer process: to give it a structure and a framework, to show you where to look, how to find your bearings and to tell you what you need to know. On the other hand, if you actually want to do any work, practical application is essential. This is so that participants can get to grips with the "tools," both physically and emotionally, to enable them to "see" with their whole body and to experience how I as the facilitator "Walk with" a participant in one single process. How well this works and, at the end of the day, the growth and further development of everyone involved is the final proof of the effectiveness of the facilitator and the method itself.

For reasons of clarity and simplicity I have dispensed with the use of separate references to the masculine and feminine at points throughout this book. But please rest assured that both are always meant.

The many examples of Walks and Family Constellations in this book all rely on my memory, as I never make any notes. I've gone to great lengths to outline the processes in the examples as accurately as I possibly can.

Finally, I would like to give my special thanks to my dear wife Anne, whose idea it was that I should write this book.

Introduction, or
How It All Began

When I was running a workshop on "Family Constellations" in San Francisco at the end of 2006, one of the participants asked me during a break if I knew of "Walking-In-Your-Shoes." I was obliged to reply that I didn't. This came as a real surprise to him, because, as he put it, the underlying feel of my workshop and the atmosphere in the role plays seemed very familiar to him. It was almost as if he had been taking part in a "Walking-In-Your-Shoes" workshop. He kept telling me that I really had to give "Walking-In-Your-Shoes" a go myself and gave me the name of Joseph Culp from Los Angeles.

A whole year passed before I remembered what the participant had told me about this other method. Normally I tend to treat such suggestions with a degree of instinctive caution, but, strangely enough, in the case of Walking-In-Your-Shoes I knew right away that I wanted to find out more about it. Something about it appealed to me strongly enough to overcome my reticence. I used the Internet to track down Joseph Culp and his workshops and training before finally enrolling directly with him for training in this method.

Author, director and actor Joseph Culp founded Walking-In-Your-Shoes together with psychotherapist John Cogswell. Since 1990 he has been offering workshops for actors and directors which bring actors and therapists together. In 1992 he founded the "Walking Theater Group." Joseph uses Walking to gain a better understanding of his roles as a TV and film actor. And the workshops he puts on for fellow actors (and aspirants to the profession) are concerned with encouraging them to use Walking to grasp their roles from "within." Every role has an inner core, and, so the theory goes, only when an actor has revealed it through Walking, really felt it for himself and scrutinized it from all sides can he then understand and develop his film or theatrical role from the inside. In this way he can embody the role with his whole being and become the person he is depicting.

Joseph discovered and elaborated on the Walking-In-Your-Shoes method in collaboration with John Cogswell. Until his retirement, John Cogswell was a psychotherapist with many years of practice behind him. He trained in humanistic-existential psychotherapy, studied C.G. Jung and, from 1982 to 2002, Buddhism under the guidance of Tibetan lama Gyatrul Rinpoche. He has been publishing works on Walking-In-Your-Shoes since 1993; more recently he has been training fellow therapists in Los Angeles and Santa Barbara in the method. From the interview with him reproduced in the appendix, it seems obvious to me that the influence of Lama Gyatrul, under whose guidance he also took the Bodhisattva vows, reinforced his experience of the unity of all beings and his ability to experience genuine empathy.

The two founders of Walking-In-Your-Shoes recognized early on that "Walking" was not restricted merely to theatrical roles but could also be applied to roles from real life, e.g. real people. It was this insight which allowed it to transcend the limits of the theatrical and acting scene, leading to the development of Walking-In-Your-Shoes in its present, more extensive form.

My first meeting with Joseph Culp took place in March 2008 in the "Electric Lodge Theater" in Venice, near Los Angeles. He was waiting for me at the entrance and the warmth of his greeting establishing an atmosphere of openness right from the outset. The photos on his website had portrayed a classically handsome, very masculine-looking man, who could just as well have worked for a model agency or played the role of the Marlboro cowboy: to me, however, he appeared perfectly normal, human and natural. We went together into the basement of the "Electric Lodge Theater," which also doubled as the theater storeroom and was clearly often used by Joseph for his Walking and theater group. In this group he teaches other actors, using Walking to help them to get to know their theatrical roles better and to internalize them. It was in this room that we met over the course of several days for one-to-one coaching sessions, each of which lasted for several hours.

Joseph invited me to sit directly opposite him on a chair. It was completely unlike anything I had imagined. He explained to me slowly and calmly what was going to happen, referring to his documents to make sure he didn't omit anything important. I was immediately struck by the fact that almost everything he was saying was familiar to me from the preparation of my own workshops in Family Constellation. He suggested that he himself should "Walk" something for me and asked me who I wanted to choose. The first person I wanted to take a look at was my father. A lot of the basics involved in the role of the "Walker," or "representative," were already familiar to me from Family Constellation work. Joseph stood up and told me that he was now going to empty his mind of other concerns until he was ready to completely commit to the process—regardless of what might then happen. Loudly and clearly he named the role he was now going to assume: "I am now Chris's father." The Walking began with the first step.

He Walked round the room in a circle. After a while, he started to talk about the things that he was experiencing in his role as my father. He spoke aloud, giving a running commentary on what he was perceiving, a kind of monologue. In this way, I heard in great detail how he was experiencing being my father in every phase of the Walk. When I started to imagine during this process that it really was my father in the flesh who was Walking around in front of me, some things became clear. I was able to learn something important from him, to understand what he found difficult, what his aims and desires were and what was causing him to suffer. This helped me develop understanding and greater respect for him just as he is and was—and what made this possible was my realization that he had no choice but to be the way he actually is

We took a break and carried on in the afternoon, and in the course of this and the coming days I experienced various interesting and insightful Walks. We Walked, among other things, me myself, my mother, my grandfather, my mother's partner, my father's wife, my underdeveloped areas and my blind spot. At times, Joseph adopted my Walking roles; at other times, I carried them out myself. In the Walk it was both exciting and moving to have first-hand experience of how my grandfather—who had been in the war but had never been able to express his view of this period, either politically and personally—had felt and to gain a direct insight into the dilemma he had found himself in (see example "Grandpa Leo").

Once I had returned to Germany in April 2008, my wife and I met up with colleagues and friends and experimented with this new method several times in small groups. We wanted to gather experience and discover the possibilities that Walking-In-Your-Shoes might have in store for us and future participants. We Walked a great number of different roles, down to and including those of homeopathic remedies such as sulphur, mercurius and natrium chloratum. And we weren't disappointed: the specific properties and effects of these on individuals really did come to light in this process, and my wife's training as a homeopath allowed us to verify them. And it's my belief that a lot of further areas of application for this method are waiting to be discovered.

I didn't initially give this method a great deal of space in my professional work as a Family Constellation therapist. To be honest, I doubted whether the method would be able even to approach the effectiveness and depth of Family Constellation work. Some time later, however, in the course of one of my regular weekend seminars, it suddenly emerged that all the issues involved with the Family Constellation had been processed after just one day. The group obviously still had a lot of energy, and we no longer had any plans for the Sunday. I then remembered Walking-In-Your-Shoes, and so I spontaneously invited everyone present to try out something new with me free of charge the following day. Half of the group wanted to go along.

I started by explaining the new method, and after this we experienced some profound and insightful Walks. I found that this generated a lot of enthusiasm and interest. The participants discovered new and interesting ways to get to know themselves and other people better. At the end, some of them asked me to consider training in the method. I asked for some time to think about it, and a few weeks later, when I actually made the decision, five of the six people who were originally involved in the experiment also enrolled in the workshop; by the time the training actually started we had been joined by further participants. This was how it all began. Walking has in the meantime become an essential element of my professional activity, both in workshops and in training groups.

In March 2009, I again met up with Joseph Culp, this time in Studio City near Los Angeles. I had been experiencing a burgeoning desire to write a book about Walking-In-Your-Shoes which had by then crystallized into a resolution, and so I wanted to interview Joseph. It became apparent that the two hours which we had allotted for an exchange of experience were way short of what we needed, so we continued the interview two days later in his apartment in Santa Monica. There, at his kitchen table, everything became much more personal; my prepared questions suddenly no longer sounded quite so prepared, and everything I wanted to ask flowed spontaneously. We became very close, and the resulting exchange was deeply personal.

The experience which I had soon afterwards and which I would like to tell you about was not planned in advance. I returned from San Francisco to Los Angeles one day earlier than planned. This meant that I could take part in one of Joseph's Walking workshops in the "Electric Lodge Theater," which was due to take place in the basement room described earlier. I was just entering the building and heading for Joseph's workshop room when the theater secretary buttonholed me to tell me that we were in line for a "Max 10" slot and asked me to let Joseph know. I already knew what this was about: The theater regularly offers regional and foreign artistes the opportunity to show their skills with a performance of their choice. Ten artistes have a maximum of ten minutes apiece to present a play, recitation, song, dance or some other kind of performance. After exactly 10 minutes a bell rings and they have to stop: hence the name "Max 10." But what I didn't yet know was that our performance was scheduled to begin in less than one hour!

When Joseph came in and I gave him the news he appeared a little nervous. It went without saying that he wanted to use this valuable opportunity to present his theater and Walking group to the general public. But nothing suitable had been prepared. He pondered for a while in silence and then said: "We should use this opportunity anyway! We'll all go on together!" Whereas the others had already had considerable experience of this kind of thing, I naturally enough wanted to know what we were supposed to present on the stage. Joseph's answer was this: "We'll all go on stage, and each one of us will do a Walk—we'll Walk the subject of 'security'. Together, we'll Walk 'security' on the stage. We've seen how worthwhile this has been in earlier Walks, because anyone who Walks 'security' also gets in touch with their own lack of security. So being confronted with your own insecurity can illuminate unknown areas within you and allow you to grow. Okay? Good luck!"

At this time there were four of us: two participants, Joseph and me. We only had 15 minutes to prepare for our performance. We all agreed on a rule that anyone who came on would only start speaking once it had become obvious to everyone that another had finished talking: this was the only way to avoid chaos. We went into the auditorium, in which roughly 60 spectators had already gathered. The theater was not very big and pretty Spartan; everything was made of wood and rather dark. It was hot. I was too wound up about the "spontaneous happening" and too excited about what was to befall me to have stage fright. Once the artiste before us had finished his very original Broadway parody, it was our turn. Joseph introduced us as a theater group which was working on a play called "Security"; we were to present what we had done so far as work in progress. We then went on stage and, as with every Walk, each of the four of us took turns to announce loudly and clearly his own role: "I am now security."

When we first started to Walk it must have looked like complete chaos. But then each of us got more and more fully into his role. I myself had the feeling that I was going window shopping, completely relaxed, with a coffee cup in one hand; Joseph later styled this "Starbucks man goes window shopping." Another participant sensed and saw her own "fetters" all around her and almost began to panic. A further Walker got into an interaction with Joseph and pulled of one of his shoes. Joseph himself took off his shirt, sat down bare-chested on the floor and began to breathe loudly. Until then he had been dogging my steps, but then the other participant's panic attack attracted my attention. I slowly approached her, asked her in a loud voice if I could help her and then, with her permission, used my imaginary sword to cut through the fetters in which she was enmeshed. She stopped to check how she was doing and let out a long, deep breath—she was feeling liberated. We then held hands and crossed the stage together. It felt good for us to enjoy her new-found freedom together, and we breathed very loudly and heavily in the same rhythm. In the process we noticed that the other two had also suddenly started breathing in exactly the same way, and all four of us went on breathing very deeply in the same rhythm. Then the bell went; the ten minutes were over, and we left the stage with applause ringing in our ears.

Wow! Down below in the workshop room a mood of euphoria swept through us, and we started talking excitedly about what we had just experienced. I would never have thought that I would ever have stood on a stage in this way—and, in the blink of an eye, the experience was behind us. The others were still pretty excited about this amazing experience, which had been nothing less than the first ever four-part Walk.

In June 2009, during my next visit to Los Angeles, I again arranged to meet up with Joseph Culp. Our plan this time was to visit John Cogswell, the other co-founder of Walking-in-your shoes, in order to conduct an interview with him too for my planned book project. I had never met John Cogswell in person, and everything I knew about Walking-In-Your-Shoes had come from Joseph Culp. Although the appointment with John had been arranged, his wife Felice had already warned us on the phone that John spoke very slowly and that, due to his advanced age (he was 85 at the time of the interview) the visit might well prove too much for his limited resources of energy. On Joseph's advice I therefore reduced my catalog of questions from 20 to 12.

John and Felice Cogswell were expecting Joseph and me for lunch at their home in Santa Barbara. We were received very warmly and hospitably. During the fantastic meal I outlined my work and talked about my intention of writing a book about Walking-In-Your-Shoes. John listened very attentively and appeared to be very supportive of my project. But it was clear that speaking was a struggle for him, and Joseph came to his aid on a number of occasions to help him formulate what he wanted to say. Nonetheless, I believe that I got the drift of what John wanted to say to us.

During the subsequent interview, which you can read in the appendix to this book, what emerged was a quite extraordinary level of warmth and intimacy, particularly when John came to tell us about "oneness." Seated between Joseph and myself, he had each of us hold one of his hands. This was exactly what *"oneness"* was about, John said. I sensed our inner connectedness and knew what he meant. I understood.

Chapter 1

What Is Walking-In-Your-Shoes?

This method, which is completely new and unique, represents a particularly striking way of developing understanding for certain people and elements, including members of your own family (either your present family or the family of origin). As soon as you develop a certain depth of understanding for a person, for their motivations and innermost being—their soul, so to speak—you will find it a lot easier to value and acknowledge them just as they are. This will promote the development of a good relationship between you, with more energy and potential—which you can also unlock within yourself. This method can also be used to help you gain a better understanding of the soul of animals. Instead of "Walking" for a person, you can do so for an animal.

When I say "Walking," that's exactly what I mean. You nominate someone in the group to "Walk" a particular person for you. This person Walks about the space, and, although you do nothing concrete or tangible, you "accompany" them with your questions about what is physically happening for the Walker. Through the process of physical movement the Walker starts to actually inhabit the role of the subject. They *become* this person and can often relate astounding stories about the experience. Unknown realities come out of concealment into plain view and start to bear fruit for you. The basic point is to make the invisible visible.

There has been a great deal of speculation about how someone acting out a role can actually sense within him- or herself something of the person being Walked. Many authors devote entire books to this topic. Unfortunately, however, none has ever come up with a really convincing explanation. I find myself in any case unwilling to go along with such explanatory models, as I'm just not particularly interested in finding

21

explanations for the inexplicable! In my view, getting to the limits of the known and staying there confers a particular power—the power that allows you to say: "I can't explain this—and that's why I don't want to try." As far as I'm concerned, knowing that it works is enough. As has already been shown, Walking-In-Your-Shoes didn't take long to grow out of its origins amongst the acting fraternity. This had to do with the insight that it wasn't only theatrical and other acting roles which could be Walked but also roles from everyday life: real people with real lives. In principle, anyone can be Walked: your mother or father, a sister or brother, a child, a deceased person, any other relative, a difficult person, a colleague, your boss, a character from the world of film or theater—and, for that matter, you yourself: your inner child, your future, your blind spots, your vocation etc. Where relationships are involved, "double" Walking—in which two people Walk at the same time and the focus is particularly on the relationship and possible interaction between them—is also an option.

With Walking-In-Your-Shoes, the whole point is to bring things to light which are otherwise concealed. We go beneath the surface to take a deeper look at certain people, animals or elements in order to arrive at a better understanding of them. On this level, which you might perhaps call the "spiritual," the person or thing is revealed in a particularly authentic and unfeigned manner. This enables me to gain an insight into how particular people tick; how they view or experience themselves in the world, what they have and what they need, their ideals and difficulties. If this opens me up to a better understanding of something or someone, I find it much easier to develop empathy and compassion and to overcome the barriers to deeper involvement. This enables me more readily to cultivate understanding and love in relation to the person, animal or element and to act accordingly in ways that will foster a harmonious relationship, both in general and in specific situations. And this also allows me to grow, because I can find out for myself how people relate to me and I to them. Many Walking roles provide answers to my questions, allowing me to get closer to an experience of myself from the "outside."

There are of course also similarities with Family Constellation work e.g. in that representatives, called "Walker," are used and we enter into a process which creates the conditions for perceiving another person in an entirely new way. Another similarity lies in the fact that we observe the Walking from the outside and, in particular, that the Walk allows us to perceive a deeper spiritual plane which reveals to us the reality as it truly is—the true character—of the person, animal or element concerned. Both processes are ultimately derived from the same source.

However, Family Constellation work differs from Walking-In-Your-Shoes in that the perspective brought to it and preparation for it are completely different. With the former, I take a systemic approach to my observations; that is, I create a kind of family tree and keep all those people who might potentially be of significance to the solution clearly in view. I look at thorny and entangled situations within the system and bring the significant persons or elements into the constellation in order to find possible resolutions. In this way, systemic conflicts spanning more than one generation can be brought to light and new approaches to their resolution applied in order to process and sort them out.

By way of contrast, with Walking-In-Your-Shoes I don't look at the whole system but rather at an individual person, animal or element. In this way I can develop a better understanding of the fears, joys, needs, suffering, desires and ideas of the other. Once I have understood what someone or something is like "inside," it becomes easier to respect them, and I can more easily find it within myself to affirm their being as it is—their whole "character" exactly as it emerges in the Walking. Esteem and respect then become the "solution," regardless of whether it is I myself, a significant person in my life or an aspect of my own being, such as a symptom, a disease or a pain that is being "Walked."

What Exactly Happens in Walking-In-Your-Shoes?

The first thing is to decide on the role of the Walker. The choice is not always immediately apparent; for this reason we sometimes need to spend a little time talking through the situation and what it is the person nominating the Walker actually wants, and I then provide assistance in determining which role is the most suitable. One of the participants is then selected to Walk this role for the person concerned. In other words, the person doesn't (for a start) Walk him- or herself but instead selects a Walker from the group. The Walker then gets ready by emptying his mind and shutting out everything that is going on around him. He or she then sets up him- or herself wholly at the service of the process, opening up fully to whatever may come, without interpretation or evaluation. The Walker repeats and names aloud the role assigned to him or her so that everyone present can hear it: "I am now ... (name of the role)."

The Walk then begins with the first step. The Walker starts to Walk, which means moving around the space. Everything else depends on, and results from, the Walker's perception of the role, both external and internal. There are no set rules, and anything can happen (for more on this see the examples). The procedure is so interesting because what is revealed by the Walk has a lot to do with the real person, real animal or real element that is being represented.

We don't know why this is the case, but it never ceases to amaze me just how closely the information which comes to light corresponds to reality and how astonished some participants are when they see how accurately a particular individual or animal is being revealed by the Walker. Even though the person doing the Walking has no conscious information about his role, he nonetheless gets incredibly close to the inner being of the individual, animal or element. Some participants have asked me how it can be that some unknown third party can be the role or subject of another person, animal or element with such precision. I then just have to admit that I have no idea. I can't explain it—and I don't want to try. The following image is all I need: Every participant brings "his" information with him in a way that is not accessible to the rational mind. Tools, such as Walking, can be used to render this information visible and fruitful (more on this in Chapter 6). Some participants have also asked me if there is a risk of getting too close to another individual and getting hold of information which he would rather not have divulged. But a Walk is just a snapshot, and what comes to light is valid only in that specific moment. Moreover, what we're doing has nothing to do with soothsaying, and so we can't presume that what we find is actually the "truth." Truth can be said to emerge from the Walk only to the extent that it brings about a positive change in the life or well-being of the participant.

At the end of the process, when something significant has come to light, it is good advice to formally release the Walker from the role. A good way of doing this is to thank his Walker and to call him again by his real first name: " You are now … again." In rare cases it may happen that a Walker is so affected by the role that he continues to feel the effects of it for quite a while, even when the Walk has long since finished and he is sitting down again. This is completely natural and has to do with the fact that the Walker has to get used to being himself again after a period of non-identification. In extremely rare cases it can happen that someone still does not manage to emerge from the role. If this happens, other specific measures can be of use, e.g., choosing a gesture of respect to make a bow before the fate of the actual person for whom the Walker performed the role. This can also be done by everybody in the group, as all the participants are united by the fact of their having witnessed the event.

Which Roles Are Appropriate?

In principle, when it comes to choosing a role, absolutely everything is possible. My sense, however, is that you will reach your limit if you choose a role which is completely outside the scope of your actual experience and has no direct significance for you. You will then run the risk of making an arbitrary choice for no reason other than mere curiosity and will need to ask yourself if this method can still be used in a meaningful and responsible manner, and also if you might not be better off using the time for another Walk. This having been said, there appear to be no limits to what can be chosen. It can make sense to choose yourself as the subject of the Walk, or your father, mother, a child or some other individual from your family. To help you make the right choice, the best thing to do is to ask the following question: "Which role can give me answers; which might be the most helpful to me in my current situation, in the present phase of my life? Which insight might help me get somewhere?" Although with Walking we are looking at the individual, individuals are still part of a system which exercises a decisive influence on them. So it makes sense when selecting a role also to look at other people from the system, irrespective of whether they are dead or alive.

What becomes apparent time and again is that our relationship with people who have passed on is not "dead": the contrary is true. Our relationship with family members, both in our own family and in the family in which we grew up, remains vital and alive. The dead have not simply "gone away": they often continue to play a major role in our lives. So, in a way, you can say that the deceased are still alive, and if you have a good relationship with them this can give you strength and make things easier for you in life. Other people who have in some significant way shaped our lives are also part of this system. These might for instance be other parties involved in an accident with us or people on whose lives we have had a negative impact.

If we have a problematic relationship with significant people, regardless of the nature of the relationship, this will be reflected in a problem area within us. We will feel its influence: in our body, behavior or views. For this reason, it can be significant to use a Walk to take a look at our relationships with living or deceased people and, where applicable, to renew them, to give them their due respect.

The chief of the Native American Pomo tribe, who opened the first US Conference for systemic solutions in Portland, Oregon, in 2005, said to those of us who had come "from the western world" something which I found very moving indeed. If I may take the liberty of reducing his long and interesting speech down to a single sentence, it is this: "I'm happy that you have finally also found a way of practicing and understanding that which has been working well for us for thousands of years … When we are in need of healing, we sometimes invoke our ancestors."

It is also possible to have former partners Walked. They are likewise part of our system and have a role to play, because they have played their part in shaping our destiny. Even if a former partner relationship may no longer be "active" because it is in the past, the connection still lives on. If we fail to respect our partnerships simply because they are out of mind, they can be a breeding ground for enormous conflicts.

You can also choose an individual from your daily life whom you find problematic, for instance, a work colleague or neighbor. This can help you arrive at a new understanding of the person in question, because someone can only be problematic for us if we fail to understand them. Gaining an insight into how this person functions can be a key to a new way of behaving—toward ourselves and other people.

Instead of Walking for a person, you can do so for an animal. This is a particularly fruitful area which has a great deal of undiscovered potential. Animals who live with people also share intensively in their lives. They have a well-developed faculty for registering very subtle currents and disruptions and are capable of perceiving emotional and spiritual events and changes. If the aim is to reach a better understanding of the life of the animal or your relationship with it, Walking can in many cases have a twofold effect. It is often only possible to help the animal by helping the person at the same time. As animals very often take on to themselves the problems and burdens of the people they live with—something which the latter often either completely fail to notice or only noticed too late—insight into some significant part of the life of the person involved is required if the animal is to be relieved of its burden. If, for instance, we recognize what the animal is focusing, this can be an important clue to what the person involved has overlooked. Once the person has solved the problem, this also liberates the animal.

It's also possible to Walk a particular part of a person, e.g. the inner child, a "blind spot" (and everyone has one) or an aspect of them that is underdeveloped. You can also Walk a vocation, an addiction, the future, self-esteem … the list is endless. What I consider universally applicable, however, is this: You can never have too much understanding!

27

The Walk Begins

The Walk begins with the first step. If the Walker first needs to get his bearings and find his way into the role, it makes sense if he just starts moving around the room—Walking in the space. But any other kind of movement is possible, and I recommend not imposing any sort of structure. Some roles are characterized by the impossibility of taking even the first step. Sometimes the Walk is defined by stagnation or heaviness; this is an important indicator, and it would be pointless to try to force a Walk into life. Sometimes, on the other hand, the defining features of a Walk are lightness and strength.

After the first few steps I check out how the Walker is Walking: that is to say, what strikes me or seems characteristic of the Walk. Is he taking long or short steps? Is he Walking fast or slowly? Is there a rhythm or pattern? Is he Walking energetically or feebly? Where is he looking? How is the Walk coming across to me? How is it coming across to the Walker himself? What is happening right there in front of me? I try to understand exactly what is happening. What is *really* happening?

The Walk gets the body moving, perhaps to a particular beat, and energy is released. The movement of the energy in turn frees up images, emotions and impressions, all of which have a lot to do with the role. These are what we want to find, to work out.

Whilst the Walker continues in his role and Walks on, I ask him what he is becoming aware of, whether images or sensations are arising and what the particular features are of the process. I try to form a picture of what is happening. I use my observations and questions to start working out the important details and rendering them comprehensible to the participant who is Walking and the rest of the group. I have to be careful not to interpret what is revealed to me but to stick closely to what is actually happening. I don't get involved in flights of imagination; instead I keep my thoughts and images close to what is directly discernible.

It's also important to pay attention to the essential elements of the Walk. I can ask the Walker what he is becoming aware of as he is Walking. For the actual purpose of the process lies in getting to the heart of the matter, in uncovering those things of true significance—and it is this, and only this, that determines the choice of questions to the Walker.

Chapter 2

Examples of "Classic" Processes of Walking-In-Your-Shoes

My work with Walking-In-Your-Shoes has over the years proved to be effective. In the processes, important insights regularly emerge which open the door to an understanding of the inner world of the person, animal or element which is being Walked. This alone is often enough to take the participant to a deeper level, encouraging the development of insight into his own inner workings.

This section is concerned with the "classic" process of a Walk if it unfolds in the way described above. This means that only one Walker is involved in the process. No further elements (such as those out of Family Constellations) are added. This is how Walking historically originated and how John Cogswell and Joseph Culp work in California. The advantage of this is that the process can remain clear and be kept relatively short, no longer than 10 to 20 minutes. This makes it possible to directly follow up with further Walking processes for the same participants and to pick up on essential elements from the preceding Walk, paving the way for further exploration. This kind of "classic" Walk with only one person Walking is often all that is required to set an inner process in motion.

It isn't always appropriate to work systemically with a Family Constellation. In a Walking process I can in a different way grasp valuable information from a more profound level of human existence. I can look more directly and clearly at important issues and individuals. This allows me more directly to examine important aspects and insights without needing to adopt a systemic view.

If you can completely and utterly surrender to this "journey," the source of the insights you can derive will never run dry. Throughout

31

my workshops and trainings I have enjoyed the gift of a seemingly boundless wealth of insights and discoveries. The great thing about all of this is that every single time—and in every process—I understand a little more about the "concrete" individual who is working with me, and about myself and my own nature.

The following examples are intended to give you a clearer picture of what is actually practiced in my workshops. Sometimes one single example says more than a whole lot of theory. I've combed my memory to commit to paper a few outstanding examples for you and made an effort to reproduce these as accurately as I can, even though I don't make notes in my workshops.

Asperger's Syndrome?

This is a Walk which Joseph Culp led in his practice room in Los Angeles, and which I myself Walked. It was a Walk in the role of a male, whom I shall call Robert.

It again began with naming the person. I said: "I am now Robert," and off I went. I walked and walked and walked for quite a long while … to start with I didn't pick up anything. I just kept going, on and on. Nothing presented itself to me. On and on—I slowly started to get anxious. I just didn't seem to be getting into the role. The Walking appeared increasingly pointless. I couldn't feel anything at all. It gradually started to bother me that nothing was happening inside and that I couldn't feel anything. But I carried on Walking just the same. Giving up doesn't seem to be in the nature of that role.

I then caught sight of a stick lying on a chair. I picked it up. As soon as I had the stick in my hand I knew that it was significant to me. I had no doubt that something important was associated with it. I just didn't know what it was, and that was what I now tried to find out. I used the stick to walk with—no, that wasn't it. I flourished it like a sword—that didn't feel right either. I wielded it like a club—no, nothing there. I tucked it under my armpit like a crutch—no, that didn't make sense either. So now I tried some completely different approaches. I held it up to my face like Pinocchio's nose—no, that was just stupid. How about a symbolic phallus, some kind of tribal artifact—nope, that was ridiculous. Or perhaps it was like a yoke for carrying merchandise, like the Chinese use? Rubbish! What about a broomstick—could I ride on it? No, nothing there. Perhaps it was an animal's tail—no, that was a complete dead end. I balanced the stick on my head, then on my hands, then at my side … in front of me … to the left … to the right … nothing helped. Until, in a flash of inspiration I wedged the stick under my right armpit whilst keeping hold of it in my right hand. That was it! I was a tap dancer! And now I was also wearing a top hat. So I started to tap-dance. Wow, I felt really alive and full of energy! I raised and lowered my hat whilst switching between tucking the stick under my arm and jabbing it into the ground. It just got better and better. I circled round the stick with a beatific smile, carried on with the dance steps, took a bow and felt a great lightness and ease. By now I was feeling like Fred Astaire, strutting his stuff with Ginger Rogers and singing. Yes, I was Fred Astaire himself, and in my head I heard the classic melodies of the great dancer's era! I felt really happy, utterly happy. And now it dawned on me how much I had after all been taking in the whole time—yes, I could do it! What earlier seemed so utterly elusive had become child's play. I felt like a hero. Everything that was gray, dull and heavy had been swept away; all that was left was pure exuberance of spirit and carefree lightness. And this is where we left it. I took my seat again.

Looking back, what we saw in the Walk was my initial extreme difficulty in developing an awareness of and feeling for the role. It had actually seemed completely impossible. It took a trick for me to open up into a state of awareness.

I know that Robert loves music and listens to music all the time, everywhere he goes. To me it looked as if music—and the imagination and energy associated with it—might be able to help him bridge the gap between his inability to feel, on the one hand, and the exuberance and joy released by opening up to something akin to feelings on the other. In the face of all his difficulties he still managed to gain access to his own inner world of emotions. This was a fantastic trick which turned this otherwise rather strange and seemingly fragile individual into someone really likeable. I now had some understanding of the difficulties Robert might be used to encountering in his daily life, of what he was missing, what made him happy and why he was always listening to music. These insights would now enable me to support him in those things that were important to him and to find a new level on which we could communicate. I also now have a pretty conclusive idea of why Robert took up tap-dancing with such enthusiasm and joy at such an advanced age.

One possible solution to the puzzle might be that he suffers from a form of autism, Asperger's Syndrome.

Addiction

One day a woman called me up and told me that she wanted to quit smoking. She asked me if she would be able to Walk the smoking issue. I talked with her, and together we explored whether the role of smoking would be able to provide the really important answers. Later, when the workshop had begun, I suggested that she might like to Walk the issue of "addiction" instead. It subsequently emerged that this was the likeliest way for her to engage more deeply with her issue.

The participant chose someone to be the Walker for her "addiction." The Walker got herself ready and said loudly and clearly: "I am now 'addiction'." She began the Walk with the first step and started to circle round the room. After a short while we could already see that, in her laps of the room, she was avoiding a particular area, so that her otherwise circular course ended up with a "dent." I asked her what was up with the part of the room that she was avoiding, and she told me that there was a barrier which she couldn't overcome. When I persisted with my questioning, she went on to say that she could actually see a river there which she was unable to cross. I asked her to take a closer look at the river and to explore it more thoroughly. She then tried to approach the river and, at various points along the "bank," to get right down to the "water's" edge. She tried it both down and upstream and told us about the bank, which was so constituted as to make it impossible to get down to the water at any point. She became increasingly frustrated because, in spite of her best efforts, she was simply unable to cross. Stuck on "her" side of the river she began increasingly to lose the initiative, and her inability to get across was progressively draining her energy. I asked her to imagine what might be on the other side of the river and to experiment with ways of crossing over to find out.

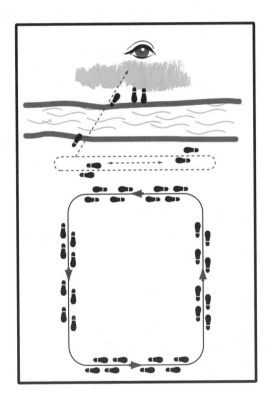

I asked her to try to imagine she could do it anyway. Stretching out one leg, she planted one foot on the "other" bank, perilously straddling the "river," before she then brought over the other leg with the result that she was now standing with both feet on the other bank. Once there, she stopped to have a look around. She reported back to the group that she was in the midst of a dense fog and was trying to get her bearings. For a while she peered intently into the fog until she caught a glimpse of something that looked like a circle. On closer observation she realized that the circle was actually a large eye. She looked directly into the eye and suddenly felt much freer. It was as if she had shed a burden. She now felt that the eye had actually been with her the whole time, protecting her, and that a profound force was emanating from it and radiating out towards her. She then turned round to go back in the opposite direction and reported that she could feel the power of the eye giving her strength and warmth from behind. She looked up and cast her gaze out to the horizon—and then all was well with her. I then brought the Walk to a close: the participant thanked the woman who had been Walking for her and took her seat again.

I talked to the participant and asked the other members of the group what they had noticed and felt about the Walk. I can summarize the experience like this: The side of the river on which the Walker found herself at the start probably represented the side associated with the addiction; the other side was free of this addiction. As long as the participant continued to smoke she was unable to cross the river, and this was a source of increasing frustration. Her smoking habit was preventing her from crossing over. As soon as she stopped smoking she would be able to cross over to the other side. There it was foggy (perhaps as an after-effect of smoking?), but she saw that growth, development, strength and knowledge (the eye) were waiting for her—a potential that was probably being frustrated by smoking: who knows, perhaps even by her fear of her own development. So now she had had a foretaste what the reward was going to be, which might help her to adjust to—and even actively seek out—the positive development in her life that would follow.

Vocation

A woman was in search of her professional future. As she had absolutely no idea of what it might be, no sense of how to move her life forward, I suggested that she get someone to Walk her "vocation." She agreed and selected a Walker from the group to Walk her vocation for her. The Walker named her role and began to Walk.

The first step was very hesitant, as was the second ... But things then started to pick up a little, although the Walk remained uncertain. She mostly kept her eyes on the ground, occasionally casting the odd quick glance in some other direction before looking down again. I asked her how she was feeling, and her reply was that there were simply way too many options. She could see far too many possibilities, and not one of them was within reach or even clearly identifiable for her. Okay, so there were a lot of possibilities, but they all seemed much of a muchness, making it impossible for her to reach a decision. I asked her to imagine looking at the horizon in order perhaps to find some kind of bearing or fixed reference point. She duly did as I suggested and observed that everything now seemed to have become *even more* difficult. She could now see a practically infinite array of possibilities, and the whole endeavor appeared completely hopeless.

I now had the idea of trying something completely different: getting her to leave the circle of chairs completely. As she could see all these possibilities from her vantage point in the middle of the circle, I was wondering what she might see from outside it. The Walker said that she thought she would be able to leave the circle. I asked her to look around to see which part of the circle would be her way out. She chose her exit point and stepped out.

Once outside the circle she stopped to find her bearings, and it dawned on her that she had never been there before. It felt like completely new territory—like something that had never been discovered. She noticed a significant change. Inside the circle it had all been simply too much for her; outside it, on the other hand, she was finally able to breathe. She got a sense of where she was and how she was. She was now in the position to see everything from "the outside," and the realization dawned that she hadn't previously been able to see the wood for the trees. Because she had always been "on the inside," she had never been able to see the picture from the outside. With her new-found perspective looking in from the outside she was now able to distinguish between the various possibilities and get a proper overview. She started to feel better and better, and we could see her strength returning. It was as if she were in a forest, breathing in lungfuls of fresh air. She breathed in and out very deeply several times. This place and the freedom associated with it were very important and full of meaning for her. She also said that, in this place, it was easy for her to establish contact with other people. She started to blossom before our eyes. At the end of the Walk she said that she wouldn't rule out the possibility at some later time of going back into the circle as long as she had spent enough time outside it.

A process of reflection, supported by the observations of the other group members, gave rise to a clear picture of this Walk. Before the participant could find her vocation she would need a completely different perspective: from the "outside." Perhaps she would be able to do something to bring about a shift in perspective on all questions of profession—to help her see and decide what she would need to do in the future. It had become clear that, from her current perspective, she had no chance of finding her vocation.

The participant liked the new idea and told the group that she thought she could now go on holiday to a place where she had been many times before. But I reminded her of what her Walker had said: that she had never been to that place outside the circle, and that she might want to take this into account in her choice of holiday destination. Who knows, I said, without a trip to some completely new place on the "outside," the new journey on the "inside" might be more difficult—or even impossible. This didn't necessarily need to be a holiday or journey at all. Anything which would get her "out of the circle" might do instead.

Ghost Train

One participant told us that she was always having difficulties with her colleague at work. There was a great gulf of understanding between them, and their relationship had been marred by a series of conflicts. So she wanted to learn to understand her colleague on a deeper level. She selected a woman to do the Walk for her.

The Walker named her role and began to Walk in large circles without venturing into the middle of the room. She was Walking in normal steps at medium speed. After a while I asked her what she was seeing, and she said this: "There are people in the middle of the room." She carried on Walking. After some more time had passed she said, "There are people lying in the middle of the room, and they are dead." This went on for quite a while, and each time she went for another lap the Walker referred to the corpses in the middle. The dead seemed to exert a particular fascination on her; she even went as far as to say that she wanted to be there with them. I asked her if she could imagine being in contact with other, living people, but she said she couldn't. "These people in the middle are the only ones I have any connection with. I don't care about the others, or anything else around me." The only people she appeared capable of loving were the dead in the middle, and her desire to join them had, if anything, intensified. This remained the case for the entire Walk. As she put it, this was the only way for her to be happy.

Collating the observations of everyone on the workshop gave rise to the following picture: the "problem" person at work appeared to feel an inner connection with a lot of dead people. Had she perhaps committed some act which had resulted in the deaths of others? It might also be that she was looking at the deceased from her own family of origin and felt connected with her own family system through her inner connection with the dead.

It seemed that it might be too much to expect her to be able to move towards the living (her colleague and other people) and to give them her full attention. What seemed more likely was that she preferred to

39

close herself off from human contact, and anyone looking to establish closer contact with her was going to be disappointed. And yet, if the participant wanted to understand her or even develop a friendship with her, it seemed that a possible method might be to respect and affirm her love for the dead. This would make it easier for the colleague to move towards her, perhaps allowing something new to emerge or a small chink in her defenses to open up.

Sore Feet

One participant was complaining of sore feet. They always took so long to heal, she told us, and she was hoping that Walking might give her a clue as to the cause. One of my students, facilitating the Walk on my behalf, asked the participant to choose someone to Walk "the feet"—"her feet." She selected a woman to do the Walk for her.

The Walker set off, and we could see straight away that she was Walking in a very gingerly fashion. Her steps were very, very slow and measured, just like those of a cat on the hunt. At the same time we could also see that she was putting her feet forward very cautiously, as if she were Walking on thin ice. She was, as it were, "feeling" her way with her feet, testing the ground to see if it would support her weight. This went on for quite a while. And, because she was moving her feet so deliberately and cautiously, she was only making very slow progress. The Walk had no particular discernible rhythm: it was simply too slow. What she was basically doing was taking a series of individual steps.

The student leading the Walk asked the Walker for her impressions, and the reply came that she did indeed feel compelled to move forward very slowly and carefully. The ground on which she was Walking was not safe. She might at any moment come across a step or some other obstacle. Or she might stumble over something or fall on a slippery patch of ground. She felt the constant need to be very vigilant and careful.

My student, who had absolutely no information about the participant, asked her what she had noticed about the process so far, and she admitted that it all seemed very familiar to her. She moved like this herself because she was almost blind. One eye was completely blind, and the other had severely impaired vision. She had to pick her way forward every day just as we had seen in the Walk; moving about in the street, in unknown buildings or unfamiliar places was always a problem because of the constant threat of injury, falling or other dangers. The student then asked the participant if it wasn't very hard work getting about in this way and whether she would be better off with some kind of walking aid, such as a white stick or guide dog. The participant declined the offer, justifying this on the grounds that she was too vain to let herself be noticed in public in this way.

The facilitator of the Walk selected another representative to support the Walker, to keep close to her just like a guide dog or human companion would do. So what we now had was a double Walk. The second Walker linked arms with the first, and they began to Walk together around the room. What emerged was a completely new picture: both of them could now move freely and easily. The Walk became quick and nimble. The supporting element was happy to be able to carry out an easy task, and the Walker was able to stride forth easily and full of confidence. Both of them were quite clearly enjoying it, to the point that they didn't want to stop.

So what did we see in this Walk? It makes sense to assume that the constant need to feel for the next step was placing the feet under an intolerable strain. It's almost as if the feet were being forced to take on part of the role normally assumed by the eyes. These "extra responsibilities" were asking too much of the feet, and this extra strain was causing them to become inflamed. The best thing to do in this case seemed to be to call on the assistance of anything which would relieve the feet of this extra burden: for example, a partner or companion.

Grandpa Leo

This was one of the first Walks I ever did with Joseph Culp in Los Angeles in which I myself was the Walker: in the role of my grandpa Leo.

41

I was intrigued to see what would happen, because my own Family Constellations had already shown me that I had a very close inner connection with my grandpa—sometimes too close. He had been dead for about eight years at that point. To help you, the reader, understand this, you need to know that my grandfather had voluntarily reported for military service in the Second World War. I named the role loudly and clearly: "I am now Grandpa Leo." Joseph led the Walk.

I set off, and it didn't take long for a strong sense of dissatisfaction to register with me in the role. I couldn't initially determine the quality of this dissatisfaction. But one thing I was sure of: I was experiencing an internal conflict, which became ever more palpable as the Walk went on. I Walked faster and faster. A sense of internal contradiction was manifesting in an ever more unpleasant way, but I couldn't for the life of me say what it was. This dissatisfaction, coupled with my inability to let out and express this feeling, became almost intolerable. I became desperate but wouldn't give in. I started to look for a way of somehow approaching this ambivalence. The disquiet was just reaching an unbearable crescendo when Joseph asked: "If this dissatisfaction could speak what would it say?"

And then the scales fell from my eyes, and I found on the spot that I wanted to make a speech to the whole world! Still in the role of my grandpa, I said this: "You didn't understand us! You thought you could judge the feelings we were carrying in our hearts. Well let me tell you, you don't have the slightest idea of what we were really looking for. And I can say this with a completely clear conscience and utter conviction. All we wanted was to have a future! No more and no less. There was no way we could know what these criminals were really up to. Do you really believe that we would have wanted such a campaign of extermination—that we would have willingly taken part in one? If we'd known what was going to happen and that there would be such a war, we would all have found another way together, all of us! There's no doubt about it! The conditions [in Germany at the time] were bad, really bad. We were all afraid of poverty. There was no future and no hope to speak of. And those of you who judged and condemned us would have done the same. The conditions were extremely bad at the time. We took this on board and placed our trust in all that we had left: a more extreme political direction. We thought that this kind of radical right-wing politics might contribute to our prosperity and make a difference to our future. And, to start with, that's exactly what happened! To start with, everyone was better off, which is why we willingly went along with and supported everything that needed to be done. We had no idea where it would all lead; he didn't tell us anything about all that, and he might not even have known himself. We didn't want these criminals to place themselves above the law and common decency, to give in to an extreme lust for power and destroy everything. So I ask you again, those of you who think you can judge us, do you really think you know what was in our hearts? You say that we were all Nazis because we went along with it. Condemning us like that is cruel and wrong. You just see the end of the story and think that we somehow all wanted it. You didn't ask us and didn't want to know what really mattered to us. You have no idea just how much we hated everything that happened when things got completely out of hand. You presume to judge us, but you have no idea how we prayed for these criminals to fall from power once we had been forced to accept just how inhuman the ideas were that these megalomaniacs were acting out. We had just wanted a candle to shed light in the darkness. And now the whole house was on fire. We *never* wanted that, I tell you—you who presume to know what it was like—you who condemned us, humiliated us and continue to humiliate us. You don't think it could happen to you, because you're better than us, us 'bad' Germans. You don't think it could happen to you because you're immune from something so terrible? You don't realize that this could happen anywhere, even to *you*. And it's *because* you're convinced that it couldn't happen to you that you've let down your guard. It could happen to anyone. This time it happened to us. Who's next? Oh, not you, of course not. After all, you know what we did wrong and have analyzed and explained it all away. But there's one thing you don't know: How it really was, and what we really wanted—a future. And, I say again: you would have done the same!"

This was how my grandpa's speech ended—and I had given it myself as a Walker for him. I then came out of the role. There was a lot to process. I had to sit down and stop talking for a while. I remember my grandpa well. He was a friendly, even jolly, but somewhat reserved man. But when he sat in front of the TV and watched the news, political reports or commentaries, he could get very angry and would often hurl violent abuse at the screen. I think I now know why. He was never able to explain to the world what he thought and felt. He felt criticized, and that was painful to him because it never seemed justified. He was probably never able to talk about it. Now I could understand him better.

My insight into his inner world led the following day to an interesting encore to this Walk. When I saw that he had always felt under fire, I suddenly recognized myself in his experience. I had often felt criticized as a young man, just as he had. This was why I felt such a close inner connection with him. Now, equipped with this insight, I was able to leave him with his own fate and see that I did not necessarily have to share it.

The Stately Grandfather

One of the participants in a Walking-In-Your-Shoes training workshop of mine wanted to have his grandfather Walked. He wasn't sure exactly what the latter represented for him or his family, as the information they had was different and contradictory. The grandfather had been dead for a very long time. The Walker for the grandfather was selected; he named the role, and the Walk began.

The representative began Walking around in large circles. After a period of Walking and introspection, he said this: "I actually feel pretty well. I'm not lacking anything and I'm not in any pain." As he continued to Walk his posture became increasingly powerful and he directed his gaze straight ahead. He straightened up and Walked in a straight line. A smile spread over his face as he said: "I feel really well. I'm in fine fettle. I think the sun's shining on me!" He started to slow a little and began to Walk his laps of the room with a dignified stride. His Walk became a saunter, but one of strength and serenity, and he said this: "I'm a splendid old gent! [laughter] Don't get me wrong, I'm no better than or different from anyone else. But it's just that I really know how to live my life. I feel as though I'm just coming out of church on Sunday morning, like everyone else, and I'm tipping my hat to people and happily greeting the ladies and gentlemen around me. That's all."

I asked the Walker for the grandfather whether there was an under-developed area or "blind spot" in his experience. The Walker looked into himself. He then said this: "I can't see what I might be lacking. That doesn't mean that I'm perfect or even that I do everything right. It's just that success comes easily to me, and whatever I do tends to work out. Because I'm successful and do a lot of good, I'm highly regarded and people admire my balance and even-mindedness. It isn't easy to upset me, and people enjoy my company." Even though the Walker for the grandfather had been Walking at quite a lick for some time, he didn't seem to be getting at all out of breath. I asked him what his view was of other people, and he said: "I love people and shower them all with my blessings! I like giving, which is why people like giving to me. I wish my grandson luck and all the best for the future." At this point I ended the Walk.

It really did seem that this grandfather was completely happy in himself. He apparently felt connected with many others and was happy. Yes, you do sometimes get people like that!

As another amusing footnote to this story, the same participant had asked me in the break just before the Walk if all Walks had to be full of woes and worries or whether there might also be Walks without any obvious problems. Well, I guess this answered the question.

Walking with an Animal

It's possible also to Walk the role of an animal. In Hannover, a man and a woman wanted to find someone to Walk for the dog they jointly owned. They told me that the dog was taking up ever more space and increasingly forcing itself on them. It seemed to need more and more attention, and this was slowly getting too much for both of them. They choose a woman to represent the dog. As always in these workshops, the Walker named her role aloud, and the Walk began.

She started Walking in circles round the room, feeling her way into the role. After a while I asked the Walker several questions, but these didn't seem to be getting her anywhere or to be important. It then struck me that the representative for the dog was keeping her eyes fixed on the couple, who were themselves paying close and keen attention to the Walk. I asked the Walker what she saw when she looked at the couple. She said that, yes, she did keep looking back at the couple and that she was worried about them. I asked her what the matter was, and her reply was that something wasn't right with them. Something wasn't in harmony, wasn't flowing; there was something cut off about the two of them. She said this: "They aren't okay. I keep having to look at them and I can't relax. It's weighing me down."

I now asked the couple what they thought the dog might mean by that. They didn't really know what to make of it. However, the way the couple were relating to each other did seem to me to be a bit distant, and I wondered whether that might have something to do with it. For this reason I brought a second Walker for the "couple relationship" into the Walk, turning it into a double Walk. The response of the Walker for the dog was this: pointing to the Walker for the couple relationship, she exclaimed: "Yes, that's what's wrong!" I then asked the couple how they themselves viewed their relationship. The question took them completely by surprise, but they did admit that their relationship was in very poor shape and that they had on several occasions seriously considered ending it. The Walker for the dog said that this was exactly what she—that is, the dog—had sensed, and she was somehow relieved. To our surprise, however, she then said this: "If you have to give me away, give me to a good home. That's all I want. Then everything will be alright." I asked the couple if they would have to give away the dog if they separated. They said they would, still reeling with surprise from the unexpected twist to the Walk.

I released the Walker for the couple relationship and brought into the Walk a Walker for a "good new owner" for the dog. The new owner and the dog hit it off right away, playing happily together and oblivious to everyone else. The dog's two current owners were as speechless as they were astonished. I asked them for their impression. More with gestures than with words they indicated that they had taken on board what they had witnessed but needed first to digest and process it. We then ended the Walk.

So what had it revealed? It seemed that the dog's attention was very much drawn to the couple relationship. It didn't seem far-fetched to assume that he was looking in some concern at the relationship between his owners and that his own future seemed uncertain, both of which were probably a major source of stress for him. It makes sense to assume that he wanted to draw his owners' attention to the fact that something wasn't right between them and they needed to do something about it. And now it was up to the people involved to determine what was to happen. But there seemed to be good reason to hope that they would find an appropriate way to behave that would relieve the dog of its burden.

Chapter 3

The Family Constellation

You may well already have looked at the Family Constellations method. I assume that many readers of this book are already more or less familiar with it. However, in case you don't know Family Constellations as originated by Bert Hellinger or want to refresh your knowledge, I'm going to look again at this valuable method by recapitulating the key points. I want to do this because the two methods—Walking-In-Your-Shoes and Family Constellations—complement one another very well, even though they are clearly distinct from one another. You could say that they arise from the same source whilst both having their own separate place in the unfolding process of insight amongst the participants, although they developed separately in different parts of the world, not knowing each other.

Both methods can be completely independent and manage quite happily without each other. However, when it seems to make sense to do so, I bring elements from the Family Constellation into a Walking process (for more on this see chapter 5).

In order to make my experience with this a little clearer for you, I would like to start by introducing you to the Family Constellations method to help you see how it can be used in conjunction with Walking-In-Your-Shoes.

For a number of years I have regularly offered workshops and training in Family Constellations. Participants and students alike have learnt to appreciate the profound effect and deep insights that can arise out of the process. This seems to be to be confirmed by the fact that many of the participants recommend me to friends and acquaintances, thereby indirectly thanking me and the method. This for me is the best possible tribute.

Recent decades have seen the development of many epistemological methods, such as psychoanalysis, group dynamics and Gestalt therapy, to name but a few. From personal experience, however, I can say that I have never yet found anything better or more profound than the methods of Family Constellation or Walking-In-Your-Shoes. The latter is an essential adjunct to my work. But both methods go hand-in-hand and complement each other perfectly.

How It Works

Firstly I conduct an interview with the participant who wants to do a Family Constellation. I ask him what he wants to achieve and about important events and facts which have been or might yet be of decisive or even life-changing importance to the people in the family system. This might for instance include the premature death of a person (including abortion), guilt, suicide, former partners or people forgotten; traumatic experiences such as war often also play a role. I then choose the roles to be represented and ask the participant to set up the people or elements concerned as representatives in the room. For this he selects people from the group who are prepared to assume these roles.

I then ask the participant to arrange the representatives intuitively in the room. Acting purely on intuition the participant then arranges the representatives in a sequence that feels right to him. What is important in this process is not to think about how the representatives should be arranged or to follow any set plan. All that counts here is intuition. For the representatives themselves it is important that they prepare for what is to come and place themselves fully at the service of the role assigned to them. They should forget everything else and empty their minds of other concerns. Then they will be able to sense the information at the point where they are standing in the room. If it turns out that a representative is not relevant to the solution, he can also be released from the constellation at any time.

What is so interesting about this is that, as soon as they have been given a role and a place and after a short period of acclimatization, the representatives are able to perceive things which, remarkably enough, have a great deal to do with the real person. Irrespective of whether the real person is alive or dead, the representative can among other things give a detailed account of how the person is and what their relationship is like to other representatives in the constellation. From this I glean important information about what needs to be done and which direction I need to take in the constellation. The constellation then develops step by step. But more on this later.

I've already stated my position in chapter 1 on questions and speculation about how the representatives can possibly sense anything at all from their roles. I don't personally need any explanation and find that my position is very neatly summed up in the following quotation from Friedrich Nietzsche: "Where there's nothing to be found, you shouldn't look."

Sometimes I ask particular representatives to say a word or two to another representative. The point of this is that I can glean additional information by looking at the effects of such words. If the words have no relevance to this constellation, it follows that they will have no effect. If, however, a sentence is important, it will not only have a recognizable effect, it will also play a decisive role in developing the whole constellation. Such words emerge out of the "flux" of the constellation. They are not manipulative; they just enable us to scrutinize certain relationships. A sentence that is not true will not be accepted by the representatives.

The Essentials of Family Constellations

The essential thing about Family Constellations is that we look at the whole family system and not just at the client. If we didn't do this, it would be impossible to find a solution. It is absolutely essential to keep everyone involved in view. This is important because this work shows that—whether we like it or not—we are accompanied internally at all times by all those family members and everyone else who has in some way exerted a decisive influence on us. If we are in good touch with everyone, we will feel within us a supporting and nurturing energy.

If, however, we have a strained relationship with someone, we will not be in resonance with ourselves—and where there is no resonance, there is pain.

Everything stands or falls on the "systemic view." By this I mean the focus on systemically relevant individuals in order to identify and dissolve entanglements. As we carry about within us the person with whom we have become entangled —sometimes without our even being aware of it—clarifying and improving the relationship with them will be both beneficial and enjoyable.

A "systemic view" means looking at the many ways in which things are passed between members of a family system, how displacements occur and boundaries are infringed. This kind of work reveals time and again that everything which remains unresolved—for instance, with a particular person from an earlier generation—is taken over and perpetuated by a later generation. The "family soul" appears to establish a balance between people who belong to a system so that no unfinished business remains. When I as client have the sense that something major remains unresolved within a family system, I then also feel, mostly unconsciously, that an opportunity to re-establish balance has arrived. If I take the unresolved issue or some other burden onto myself, I can then demonstrate my love of the family and safeguard my membership of the system—especially if I haven't been able to do this in any other way. So if I haven't been capable of showing my love for certain people in the system e.g. my father or mother, I will then demonstrate my love by assuming the burden of the unresolved issue. This other, hidden kind of love has an effect just as the open, conscious and personally experienced love does, the difference being that the effect is a destructive one. The person who takes on the unresolved burden from another has a heavy load to bear and is at one and the same time in resonance with the other person but not in resonance with himself. This manifests among other ways in unsuccessful partnerships, lack of success or depression. Only when I can look at the right person and also at the burden I have taken on myself can the pain finally depart. Only when I have rediscovered my ability to feel the other kind of love will

I be able to resolve the conflict and re-establish resonance with myself. In this case, I don't need any drugs, because the pain is no longer necessary to remind me of my resonance with the other person. If, however, I were to take drugs (e.g. antidepressants) instead of reaching a solution, I would then be pushing both the problem and the solution to one side. Drugs can only alleviate the symptoms; the cause, however, remains and will in time manifest ever more strongly. Every difficulty comes with its own inherent potential solution. But if I choose to anesthetize the messenger of the solution, it will slip away from me. The problem or burden will not finally yield until I understand why it was necessary, what it represented and why I needed it for a certain period of time.

In order to prevent misunderstandings, however, I would like to add that the use of appropriate drugs for the alleviation of symptoms within a particular context, for a particular purpose or as an emergency measure for a limited period of time can sometimes be completely appropriate.

Merely because separate people have separate bodies and tend to feel separate between themselves and others, many of us consider the distinction between "me" and "you" to be a given. Whilst it may appear obvious that we as individuals are different from one another and perceive ourselves as separate, within a community brought together by fate—within a family—the boundaries become blurred, and these distinctions cease to be quite so clear. Sometimes it's no longer possible to say where the boundaries are: Where does your life stop and where does mine start? Where does your problem stop and where does my problem begin? This is what we call systemic entanglement.

The point of Family Constellations is to make such systemic entanglement visible, so that what was previously lurking in the shadows can fully come to light. The representatives can bring this about because they are capable in a completely unbiased way of perceiving the important connections—and separations—at the heart of the system. This is the actual essence of Family Constellations.

In all the constellation work that I know there are a few essential characteristics or aspects which appear to be universal. The first of them is this: everyone has his or her own place in the family system. This place is a hereditary place which is reserved only for the person concerned. No one else can occupy this place in the long term, even if he tries to do so (and people always do try). And the second is this: If someone is unable or unwilling to take his place or is in some way prevented from doing so, then the entire system erupts into chaos. The consequence of this is that another family member—usually one from a subsequent generation—tries to re-establish balance. As all family members partake of the same "family soul," they all have knowledge of the entire system. If one individual notices that another has not taken his ancestral place or something has remained unresolved, this individual feels inwardly under pressure and believes that he has to do something to re-balance the system. This internal pressure exposes the person concerned to the conflict that arises from taking something on from another person and perpetuating it in order to fill the hole in the system left by that person so that something may come to fruition. In this way the latter takes on the feelings of the other person and actually starts to live their life. He is then no longer himself. Only when this entanglement has been dissolved and the other person has come back into conscious awareness—and is thus re-membered—can the person affected find his way back to his own being ("taboo issues" are not excluded from the process). You will find a series of examples of this in the next chapter.

Chapter 4

Selected Examples
of Family Constellations

The best way of explaining Family Constellations is to let the practice speak for itself. This is where the method proves itself, and this is also where its application to concrete situations and people is demonstrated. In the following I want to describe some examples which I find particularly noteworthy and which have stuck in my mind. I have described the constellations in a way that leaves out all unnecessary padding. In other words, for the sake of simplicity, I have left out all the paths which did not lead to a solution and those all representatives, elements and information which were not relevant to the solution.

Free-Time Family

Close to San Francisco I worked with a man of about 55 years of age. He was a Frenchman by birth, a successful businessman and broker. His issue was that he often felt ill at ease in his professional capacity, sometimes as out of place as a 10-year-old boy would be in his situation. He had had a lot of professional opportunities which he had not made use of because he sometimes felt like a fraud pulling the wool over people's eyes. He was unable to explain this because he never went behind anyone's back and merely tried honestly to do his job. He had revealed a lot of talent in his work and was very able to focus, which was why he was very much sought after in professional circles. But because all of this felt in some way "dishonest" he didn't want to take any offers that might further his professional advancement. We formed the constellation: the issue (the sense of being ill at ease) and the man, using a separate representative for each.

The representative for the man was extremely focused and alive in his role. He could see everything very clearly and was very present and attentive. However, he was unable to "see" the other person, the representative for the unease. When this other person was asked what he perceived, he said to the representative for the man: "You know who I am. You know exactly who I am. You know it. If you can remember who I am, you will have found the solution." I asked the man if he knew which person or persons might be concealed here—persisting with my questioning, I asked him, "So who might still be important or significant to you without your being aware of a direct relationship to them?" He thought about it. There were his grandparents who had been forced to flee in the war, an aunt who had emigrated to America, and there was an Italian family in his home village in France with which he had spent nearly all his free time between the ages of eight and 12. He hadn't thought about this family in ages, but his face lit up perceptibly when he spoke about them: they had been poor but warm-hearted and kindly.

I was interested in bringing this family into the constellation in order to see what kind of effect this would have. I selected one single representative to represent all of them and asked the participant to set him up. As soon as the family was in position, the representative of the man immediately began to play hide and seek with the family, just like a child. What resulted was a pretty full-on game which both parties thoroughly enjoyed for some time. During a break from this game, the representative for the man spent some time reflecting, and it occurred to him that this very short, free and spontaneous play had made him very happy, and that he now felt very well, refreshed and light in his being.

I asked the participant for his impression, and he confirmed that this had been exactly his experience! The children from this family had been somewhat older than him, but that hadn't stopped him having a great deal of fun with them and other children from the neighborhood and playing boisterous, lively and "timeless" games. His own parents had been bakers who were, in comparison to the Italian family, pretty prosperous. However, as a boy at home with his parents, the man had been bored to death. It had been so boring that he had just stared out of the window and counted passing cars for hours at a time. Time spent with the Italian family, however, had been characterized by high spirits and emotional warmth, and he had always felt very safe and at home with them.

I set up the two representatives for him and the family opposite one another. The representative for the family said, "We were always happy to give to you, even though we didn't have much ourselves. We treated you like our own son. I don't think you even noticed that you were a child of the suburbs. You weren't aware that you were rich, and we were poor. But that didn't bother us. We still gave you everything we had and were happy to share everything with you."

The representative for the man replied: "The time spent with you was the happiest time of my life. When I was with you I felt secure and protected. It was never boring with you; with you, I was able to develop. I am more grateful to you than I can possibly say. I actually have to admit that I feel a bit guilty. You are poor but gave me everything; we are rich but didn't give you much at all. I owe you something."

I understood what was going on here. The man's soul was laboring ever more intensely under the imbalance from this period. He had been greatly enriched inside by all that he had received, whilst the family had only given and was materially poor. Now, much later in life, he was unable to enjoy his success because he sensed how much of it was down to this family and his happy childhood. His soul could feel the necessity of a return to balance, which was why it felt so ill at ease. He wasn't interested in yet more success, because that success would merely reminded him even more vividly of the imbalance. His soul felt transported back into this happy time, when he was about 10 years old, and this was because there was some unfinished business from this time. As the balance had not yet been restored, he had the feeling of being a fraud, who was only taking without giving back in return.

I suggested that he might find other ways of re-establishing the balance, for example, doing something so that other people would be able to profit from and partake in the things that had enriched him so greatly. In this way, he might be able to re-establish balance and at the same time give powerful expression to his gratitude and appreciation for the Italian family. My proposal really resonated with him. He told me that from his parents, the bakers, he had inherited his rational business sense and clarity, and, from the Italian family, love, emotionality and kindness. He felt "full to the brim" and was just waiting for an opportunity to give of his fullness. He also felt that he would be unable to make any further progress in his profession as a broker and had already given up his job. He had already prepared himself for what was to come, for something new, without even knowing what it actually was. Now, he told me, it was finally time to do what he had always wanted to do but had been too preoccupied to get around to: to pass on his knowledge and skills in workshops and seminars in order to help other people. Now, after the constellation, he felt that he was both ready and sufficiently focused to do so. This activity, which will help him develop, is a powerful one which will in due course restore a harmonious relationship with those things in his life of true significance.

The Mother in the Mirror

One participant was feeling depressed and listless. The place where she was living, where she had been brought by a husband whom she was later to divorce, felt confined and lonely. She didn't want to live there any more but could see no way of getting away; nor did she know where she should go. In our interview she told me, among other things, that her mother had suddenly and unexpectedly died when she was younger. I let her select a representative for herself and her mother.

As soon as the places had been assigned and the representatives were in position, one thing became very clear: They were standing in such a way as to be able to see each other in the mirror. In other words, they were both set up with body and face turned to the mirror which hung over the wash basin in my practice room. If they had really wanted to look at one another they would have needed to turn their heads; they were instead looking at each other in the mirror some distance away.

This seemed to be somehow meaningful for both of them, but it felt a bit odd. The representative for the daughter told us that the reflection of the mother was somehow threatening—almost as if the daughter could both see and not see her mother. There was something unreal about it, even though the image in the mirror was completely clear. The mother was in her turn completely captivated by the mirror image of her daughter. She stared at it without moving and remained silent for a long time. But you could see that there was something in the mirror which had her in its grip. She struggled to find the words to describe what she was seeing and feeling. Then, as she continued to look at her daughter in the mirror, she stammered out the following: "Yes, I can see you … I can really see you. You're really there … if I can see you, you can't be far away … I can almost reach out my hand and touch you … there just has to be a way back … I've got to get back somehow … I must have got lost! And I can see you: you're there! There you are, there. And that must be the way … that has to be the way I have to go [getting more desperate] I can see the way. I can completely see the way. That's where I have to go. But that's impossible! I can see where I have to go: But that's where I've come from. But that's where I've come from!"

I knew that when people suddenly and unexpectedly die it can sometimes happen that they continue internally to cling to a state between life and death. They grasp after and cling to the living, sometimes literally, almost as if they don't know that they are dead. No matter how weird it sounds, because it is so far outside our direct experience, some of the deceased souls want to carry on being with the living, as if they were still alive themselves. Now I wanted to put this assumption to the test. I had the mother say to the daughter: "I am dead." For the mother, this felt really odd. She said quite quietly, as if talking to herself: "Am I dead?" Followed by: "I just thought I was lost. I just wanted to get back. Back to my child!" So it was true. I now got the daughter to say this: "Mum, you're dead." The representative of the mother mulled this over for a long time. Then the two of them turned to face one another directly, and the mother said this: "Yes, it's true. I am dead. I'm sorry that I tried to find my way back to you. It must have confused and frightened you. Now I'll stay here and you are there. I am dead, and you're alive. I give you my blessing for your future." The daughter answered: "Yes, I felt that something was clinging to me. Now you are there and I am here. Thanks for letting go of me. Now I can get on with my life in freedom. Thanks for your blessing." At this point I ended the constellation.

It's often been my experience that the dead cling to the living. This of course confronts us with our preconceptions: that, when we die, either everything ends or, depending on what we have done, we end up in heaven or hell; whatever happens, we are no longer there. In my experience, however, that isn't always true. People used to lay grave-stones flat on the graves themselves in order to prevent the dead from climbing out so that the living could be left in peace. Why do people need such a massive weight of security? They're obviously afraid of the dead who have not yet found their peace. Such "undead" can be neither seen nor comprehended by the living. Some people hear voices or see "ghosts." In such cases, they are often experiencing a particular kind of clinging on the part of the dead.

But why are we so afraid of this? What is it about horror movies that frightens us so much? My answer is this: these things impinge on central areas of our inner systemic reality, and we unconsciously believe that such spiritual entanglement is possible. As long the assertion that the dead cling to the living continues to be denied or dismissed as lunatic ravings, the clinging itself will remain. This is how "ghosts" come into being. If, however, we look more closely at the clinging itself, these ghosts may leave.

Twin Brothers

In a workshop in San Francisco I worked with a male participant of about 30. His issue had to do with his relationship with his twin brother, who was not himself present. The participant was unable to understand why his twin brother didn't want to have any contact with him and was looking for a solution to bring the two back into harmony. I found this issue particularly curious because twins often sense a very strong mutual connection with each other, and this connection is usually an unbreakable one. I asked him to select two representatives for himself and his brother and to set them up. Whilst he was doing this I noticed a slight air of aggression about him.

The constellation began, and the representatives slowly got into their roles. After a while, it became increasingly evident that the representative for the participant was gradually getting more aggressive, whilst the representative for his brother was at the same time becoming increasingly depressed. In the course of the constellation, the former became ever more bellicose whilst the latter retreated into an ever smaller space. The representative for the participant looked scornfully at his "brother," saying things like: "Come on, stand up properly. What a weakling you are!" The representative for the other twin continued to retreat physically until he was lying on the ground with his body and face averted from the other. When I asked how the twin brother was doing, he answered, "Please get him to leave me alone; I'm scared of him."

These were interesting and clear indications. By this point I was asking myself if we were seeing an perpetrator/victim dynamic with the two brothers, because one was behaving like a perpetrator and the other like a victim. So I asked the twin brother who was present if there was a dynamic which was the same or similar in his family of origin. He answered that his mother a few years previously had a fatal accident. There was also considerable doubt as to whether it had really been an accident or whether somebody had been involved. At this time his own father had been behaving oddly, and there was a suspicion that he might have had something to do with the accident.

I asked the participant to set up a representative for the father of the two brothers. He placed him turned away from the brothers at some distance. It immediately became apparent that the representative for the participant was behaving yet more aggressively and the representative for the brother was retreating even more into himself and just didn't want to be there any more, to the point that he would rather just disappear or even die. The father told us that he had the feeling of slowly moving away from everyone else. He had the feeling, he told us, that he was now facing his own "consequences" and was completely wrapped up in himself. He didn't want to look at his children.

I had a suspicion. Once, when watching an old video from a workshop with Bert Hellinger, I saw in a constellation that the two children of a murderer had assumed the opposing elements of his deed through their family system: one had taken on the perpetrator role and the other that of the victim. When it comes to murder, the real situation is often similar: The victim can't say anything, and the perpetrator conceals the deed. Both the concealment and the repression weigh very heavily, because their influence means that the right place in the system is no longer available. In this way, one of the most difficult cases of "unfinished business" and guilt arises. As, however, the family system doesn't absorb this guilt but passes it on, the children—that is, the next generation—come internally and unconsciously under pressure to take this unfinished business onto themselves. As long as the roles of perpetrator and victim remain in the dark and are hushed up, they will be represented by other family members. So it was that one of the children on the video had assumed the role of the perpetrator and the other the role of the victim. In other words, the children had taken on the feelings of the actual people and were expressing them toward other family members and the world in general.

This seemed to me to be what was going on in this present case as well. There were strong indications that the father really might have felt guilty for the death of his wife. But this didn't necessarily make him a murderer. He might also have been feeling guilty for not having done everything possible to prevent the accident which befell his wife. (It's important to mention this perspective here in order to avoid the risk of judgment or prejudice.) I now wanted to introduce greater clarity into the constellation and asked the representative for the participant to stand in front of the "father" and look him the eye. The participant himself became ever more aggressive; it was all he could do to remain seated. I suggested to the representative for the participant that he address the following words to the father, which he then did with utter conviction: "If you are guilty, I'll leave the guilt with you. That's your business. I'm not going to get involved in things that only affect you. So if you're now facing the consequences, you have my complete consent. I'm now going to my brother. Thanks for everything you've given me. I'm happy to be able to pass it on." The father, whilst seeming very preoccupied, now directed his gaze into the middle distance but gave his consent and wished his son all the best.

The other brother seemed to be in a better state; he began to pick himself up off the floor. I had the representative for the participant look his brother in the eye again. Both of them now looked a bit more relaxed. I heard the representative for the participant say to his "brother," "Now you don't need to be scared of me anymore. I left it all with dad. I'm sorry if I hurt you. From now on I'm only your brother." He went to his brother and helped him stand up. They looked at each other as if sizing up how profound the implications of this new insight were, and then they embraced. The participant appeared relieved and his aggression seemed to subside.

My suspicion had become stronger. It really did seem to be that one of the brothers had assumed the role of the perpetrator and the other the role of the victim. One of them was aggressive and arrogant and possibly had a closer internal relationship with the father; the other one was depressive and timid and perhaps more closely connected with the mother. So the brother in the role of victim was afraid of the other brother in the role of perpetrator—almost as if the perpetrator-brother wanted to kill the victim-brother. This meant that the two brothers were not looking at themselves at all but at the actual perpetrator (the father?) and the actual victim (the mother?). At the same time the brothers were trying to perpetuate something that was unfinished. But, as it was their parents' business rather than their own, the whole enterprise was doomed to failure. Things would be unlikely to improve for anyone involved without an attempt on the part of one of the brothers to respect and love the actual perpetrator and the actual victim.

Nail in the Wall

The following is an account from a further Family Constellation which I led in San Francisco. I was working with a participant who was having professional difficulties. He told me that he was a seller of services and admitted that he found it very difficult in conversation with customers to highlight and present the advantages of his products, even though he himself was quite convinced of them. He found proper sales patter almost impossible because he couldn't find the right words and wasn't able to show his products in a positive light. He also told me that he was fully qualified in his profession and knew everything he needed to know.

I asked him to start by selecting a representative for himself alone and placing him in the room. The participant selected a man and set him up close to the edge of the room so that the latter—who had been placed at a slight angle to the wall—was obliged to look at the wall. I gave the representative a lot of time to find his way into the role. As the representative continued to look at the wall, it looked as if he had fixed his gaze on it. I had the impression that he was focusing on a particular point on the wall. When I asked him how he was doing and what he was noticing, he said dryly, "There's a nail in the wall." Okay, I thought, so where was this taking us!? He went on to explain, "All I can do is look at the nail on the wall. It's meaningful to me. Somehow it is significant for me." The representative then reached out his hand, took the nail between his fingers, drew it out of the wall and held it up in front of his face, for all the world as if he had never seen a nail in his whole life. He scrutinized the nail attentively from all sides, almost as if he wanted to assess the effect it was having on him and what he was supposed to do with it. Then, fully absorbed, he said this: "It's a weapon. This nail is a weapon." I asked him to tell me more about it. "It's quite clear," he went on to say. "If the nail is in my hand, it's a weapon. If the nail is in the wall, it's a tool!"

At this point I still didn't have the slightest idea where this journey was taking us and didn't know what it was all supposed to mean. But it was obvious to me that something very important was manifesting very clearly here. I now asked the participant himself what he was noticing. He was also completely at a loss. I asked him where it might make sense to look for a tool or a weapon in his own life or that of his family of origin or in both. In response, the participant said that the whole "weapon" business reminded him of his father. His father really had the gift of the gab and used words as weapons. He could work magic with words, as a skilled swordsman might wield a sharp sword, and also used them to inflict serious injury. Furthermore, his father had often told lies if it was to his advantage to do so. He had also frequently lied to his wife, the participant's mother, something which the son found particularly painful. So his relationship with his father had always been very bad.

I now had an idea. Might it be that the son was unwilling to use words because they had been used against him as a weapon? Might it be that he no longer wanted to turn this weapon on others because he knew how much harm it could inflict? Was it really just a matter of distinguishing between words as weapons and words as tools? At this point I also got a representative to stand for the father. I then turned the representative for the son to the father so that they could look at each other. I wanted to see if the representative would confirm my picture of events or not. I offered the following sentences to the representative for the son, which he then repeated with utter conviction, with the effect that they sounded completely authentic: "You are my father. It was sometimes hard for me to bear the brunt of your words like blows from a sword. And I didn't want to inflict this pain, which I know so well, on my customers. I am now giving your destiny and your way with words back to you. This only makes sense in your life. Please look kindly on me if from now on I use words only as tools. Now I can really make something of my job, and, if from now on I'm only going to use words as tools, the time of words as weapons is over, even between us." The representative for the father said that he didn't feel very powerful and hadn't even noticed that he was hurting his son so badly. He then added this: "It's okay for me if you only use words as tools. If you now want to use words as tools, you can use them confidently and skillfully, just as I did. I give you my blessing." The two representatives and the participant himself looked visibly relieved. The participant said that the issue had now become clear to him that it all made sense. I let him keep the nail as a souvenir.

Sex Change

This constellation I did for a male participant from Texas. He was complaining of having no interest in sex. This problem had already broken up a few relationships, even though he had nothing against sexual intercourse per se. Even before the act took place, a feeling of something like disgust would arise in him, causing his desire to wither away. We set up two representatives: one for the participant himself and one for "sexual intercourse with his girlfriend."

Once the representatives had been set up, they felt their way into their roles. Both were so placed that they could not see each other. The representative for the participant then said that he was feeling ill at ease because he knew that somebody else was there (meaning the representative for sexual intercourse) but he couldn't see them. In order to find out how the two related to each other, I turned both representatives to face one another. When the representative for the participant looked at the "sexual intercourse" he found this unpleasant and felt very unsure of himself. He told me that he was feeling very "spongy," and not like a proper man at all. I asked the participant what was coming to mind, and what cropped up was his father. He told me that his father had always sought out women who either weren't interested in sex or weren't capable of having sex. He expressed the opinion that his father had only had sex a few times in his whole life.

I then added some others to the constellation: the father, masculinity and femininity. I asked the representative for the father first to look at the masculine. The father looked at it with obvious scorn

66

and observed that he was seeing images of drunken yobs staggering out of the pub, scratching their behinds and shouting. For him, masculinity was loud, aggressive, dirty, smelly and tasteless. I then got the father to look at the feminine. Straight away the father said this: "That's where I want to go. That's where I belong!" It was as if he were identifying squarely with the feminine. He went over to the "femininity" representative and paused briefly to reflect before turning back to us and, beaming happily all over his face, making this declaration: "I've got something to say that's really important to me and that I feel very strongly at this moment. I am now a woman! I've just got to be open about it: I'm now a woman. It's as if I can really feel myself putting on a wig and applying lipstick. That's what makes me feel good. That's what I want to be. Just that. Now everything's fine. Now I'm at peace."

The participant was telling us that this made sense to him. Things were becoming clear to him, and some of the stuff about his father had now started to make sense. In place of his representative, I now brought the participant himself into the constellation. The representative for the father then said this to his son: "I'm now a woman. That's what makes me feel good, and now I'm at peace. But even if I'm now a woman, I'll always be your father, and you can always have me as your father. Whatever happens, you will always be my son. No one can take that away from us. For a long time I wasn't aware of my sexual identity. That has nothing to do with you. As a man, you can go look for a woman and be happy. Then all three of us can meet up, and she can give me some make-up tips." We laughed. Then the son said to the representative for his father: "Thanks, dad, for being so clear. I've never felt attracted to men, but I couldn't be with women either. Now I can see that this is your business. I'm now giving the sexual insecurity back to you. And, as a man, I'm going to get myself a woman and be happy with her. I respect your destiny as it is for you and am now going to take control of mine." The representative for the father added that he now had a completely clear picture of how things were going to develop. Every time he met his son in future he was going to meet him dressed as a man. After the meeting he would put his women's clothes back on.

Much became clear to the participant, and he felt as though he had been given a gift. But I asked him not to talk to his father about the constellation. After all, we didn't know whether the father would really be prepared to look at this issue or even to talk about it. It might be that he would never take this step on his own initiative. I said that it was enough for the participant himself to find a solution and to leave everything else to his father. Only then, with this new inner view, would movement be possible, and it would take its time.

Compulsive Masturbation

Another participant from Texas came to me to ask for my advice. He told me that he was suffering from a strong compulsion to masturbate. As this extended also to public masturbation, he had previously been imprisoned for offenses against public decency. He now wanted finally to look more closely at the whole issue with the aim of overcoming the compulsion because it was destroying his life. We created the constellation, with representatives for him and for "masturbation."

The participant set up the representative for masturbation to the left alongside his own representative, relatively close, no more than 18 inches away. Both were looking in the same direction. After a while I became aware of a regular, almost rhythmic but very slow movement on the part of the representative for the participant. He was turning toward the representative for masturbation, then turning away: toward, away, toward, away. This was quite striking. I asked the participant for his own view of what we were seeing, but he couldn't yet make any sense of it. I asked some questions about his systemic background. He told me, among other things, that he had been adopted. He went on to say that he had only met his biological father a handful of times; he had, however, never set eyes on his birth mother even though there had been opportunities for him to do so. The reason he gave for this was that he hadn't got round to it.

I now asked him to set up a representative for his biological mother. He placed her to the right of his own representative and facing in the same direction. All three were now lined up facing in the same direction, with the participant's representative the middle. The latter was still making the same slow movement: turning toward the representative for masturbation then turning away: toward, away, toward, away. I asked the representative about his experience, and his reply was that he had initially felt compelled, as if out of habit, to constantly turn to his left toward the masturbation representative. But this had now changed with the arrival of the mother on the scene. His experience was now that he actually wanted to turn toward the mother but just didn't dare look in her direction. This was why he kept turning instead to the masturbation representative. In other words, the impulse was to turn to the right to the mother but the representative felt that his attempt to look in that direction was being blocked, which was why he kept turning instead to the left. He said, "It's so hard to turn to the right, but turning to the left is really easy." Masturbation felt like a good friend to him. This kind of consolation was free and always available to him. Unlike a drug, you don't have to go somewhere to get hold of it, it's legal and always there when you need it. To the right, however, there was nothing but completely unknown territory—and this explained the representative's movement: the mother was "out of bounds," so he had to keep turning to the left and back again ... the mother was "out of bounds," so he had to keep turning to the left and back again ... and so on and so forth.

At this point I developed a suspicion. It looked as if the participant was using masturbation as a substitute for looking at his mother. I asked him to turn to his mother, to stand in front of her and look her in the eye. At this point the representative became very sad. He told me that he was for the first time feeling all the pain of separation, and it was as if he was for the very first time looking at his mother—his *real* mother! He then spoke to her: "I miss you so much. I never realized how much I miss you. But now I have found you again in my heart and made space for you there." The mother's answer was this: "That's good, my son. I give you my blessing." And this is where we left the constellation.

This brief constellation had shown us a great deal. It looked as if the participant was looking for intimacy and connection with his biological mother and was missing her dreadfully. And because he wasn't conscious of this, he was avoiding going there because it was too painful to bear. Every time he tried to look at his mother he started to feel the pain in advance and "decided" instead to avoid looking at her at all. This explained why he was turning to his left—to where distraction was to be found: a means of forgetting, like a drug. But if he instead chose to look within at his biological mother and to feel the pain, he might be able to get over the pain and re-establish a sense of intimacy with her. Perhaps, I thought, it was finally time for him to meet her.

Indian Bodyworker

Back again in San Francisco a young man of about 26 asked me for advice. He was finding it incredibly hard to concentrate for any period of time. Sometimes, anything over 10 minutes was just too long. It got particularly bad when he had to sit down at his computer and do something like submit his tax declaration. He could pay attention for about 10 minutes before his ability to concentrate completely deserted him. After that, it was hopeless. This made me wonder exactly where his attention went after deserting him. I asked him to set up two representatives: one for himself and one for the "place where his attention went."

He set up the two of them some considerable distance apart and facing away from each other. First I asked his own representative for his impressions. The representative appeared restless and told me that he felt incredibly full of life. He could feel all the parts of his body very precisely and had a very strongly developed sense of "bodily awareness." He could feel his feet, his legs, his abdomen, his hands, his arms, his upper body: it was as if a pulsating, vibrant consciousness was passing through the various parts of his body. And, as it was passing through, the part of the representative's body concerned would vibrate and shake. He told me that he simply wasn't aware at all of the other representative.

I asked the participant what was going on for him, and he told me that he was a "body worker" or, in other words, a trainer in a gym. He had a view of himself as very strongly focused on his body and on exercise. Even as a student at school he had often not wanted to eat his sandwiches because to do so would have left him less time to play basketball and baseball with the other boys. I asked the representative for "place where his attention went" what he was feeling. He told me that he was feeling very happy, and he looked it. As he put it, he felt that he was in the right place. It was as if he were standing at the bank of a river in the middle of a pristine natural landscape. He had been fishing and was about to go hunting. He felt fully at one with nature and in exactly the right place. Everything was "flowing," and he felt totally happy. His place in nature and experience of harmony with his natural surroundings was making him feel secure and connected with everything around him. He was at the same time, just like everything around him, totally relaxed, and everything was in complete harmony.

I once again asked the participant himself for his impressions. He told me that he was experiencing a clear sense of his Native American roots. His four grandparents were from four completely different ethnic origins: One of them was Russian, one Filipino, one Latino and one Mexican-Indian. He told me that he loved being out in nature, fishing, hunting and simply being free. This meant a great deal to him, and he took every single opportunity to get out of town.

I now asked him to set up his Native American tribe. He placed this representative close to the enormous Buddha figure in the room (my seminar room in San Francisco was in a Buddhist meditation center, and every room contained a Buddha statue). I then asked the representative for the participant to turn to and look at the representative for his Indian tribe. It didn't take long for the representative for the participant to become very sad and even a little angry, and he said this to his tribe: "What's become of you? It makes me really sad to look at you—I find it really painful. I can see that everything is in ruins. What's become of our pride? What's become of our culture? What's become of our ancestors? What's become of our land? And what's become of

71

our ability to enjoy life??? I just can't accept that everything is gone for good. I'm going to fight to put everything back in its place, so that you and my ancestors will be pleased with me." Having given this speech, he suddenly felt strong.

Now I turned to the representative for the tribe and asked him for his impression. He was quiet for a long time and kept his gaze fixed on the floor. Then he slowly began to speak: "My boy ..."He said, "My boy ... you are brave. That's good. You have a good heart. That's good too. But you can't change our destiny. You can't turn us into something other than what we are. You aren't going to be able to save us. Nor is there anything that you could or should save, because we just are what we are. We will always be what we are. Our spirit is alive. It's alive even in you and will never be lost. Our spirit is immortal. It's immortal in you too. Be proud of what you have and what you are, and leave all the difficult stuff with us. Don't get involved in what is past; take it into the future and let it develop. That will make me proud of you. Pass it on to your children and teach them our traditions as well as you can. If you do that, I will always be with you."

That really hit home! The participant was greatly moved and told us that he understood exactly what was going on and where his blind spot had been. Even though he had been unaware of his systemic entanglement, a clear way forward had presented itself to him. And this is where we left the constellation.

In the constellation it became clear just how badly the participant had been missing this particular one of his many roots and how it had been concealing some unfinished business. Looking at it had enabled him to get to grips with something really significant. It would seem reasonable to assume that every time his attention deserted him when he was trying to concentrate, it was wandering off in search of his Indian roots. And the unfinished business there was literally forcing itself on him.

A few months later both of his parents registered for a Family Constellation with me because they also wanted to experience the relief and release from which their son had so strongly benefited. They told me that the constellation had had such a marked effect that their son was now significantly more able to concentrate, with a knock-on benefit for his life and career. Once out of the starting blocks, there was no stopping him.

Portal to a World of Dreams

A woman in her mid-forties from San Francisco was looking for answers to help her find a new relationship. She was finding it hard to approach men or even to register their existence, even though she was interested in men rather than women. So she had hardly ever been in a relationship, even though she wanted one.

We set up the constellation: the woman and a potential partner. She placed the potential partner's representative close to the center of the room. Her own representative was set up at a point in the room where the wall jutted out, so that, although she wasn't in the corner, she was nonetheless looking at a white wall. I asked the representative for the potential partner what he was feeling. He told me that, although he was definitely attracted to the woman, he had the impression that the woman had not noticed that he was there. She was thoroughly wrapped up in herself. I then asked the representative for the participant about her experience. She was feeling a bit bemused and first needed to get her bearings. While she was doing that she carried on looking at the white wall. It took her quite a while to notice what was actually happening to her. She told us that she was finding it hard to register anything at all; at any rate, she was unable to take any note of the representative for the partner. It was almost as if everything that wasn't connected with the wall wasn't real, that nothing else existed. There was just the white wall and nothing else! She continued to stare fixedly at the wall in front of her. She then reported that the whiteness of the wall was beginning to change: It was beginning to flicker and blink, rather like a TV screen. The "screen" gradually became ever more real, and after a while the representative said that it felt as though she were watching TV. She could see things on the screen as if they were in a distant country, and a procession of interesting scenes presented themselves as she watched. There were strange people and landscapes which appeared to be telling a story just like in a fairy tale. What gradually emerged was an entire "dreamscape."

I asked the participant for her impression. She replied that the experience her representative was relating to somehow seemed familiar. As a child she had devoured books. Even in the summer, when other children were playing outside, she had preferred to sit in her room and read. Her parents had been concerned that their daughter spent so much time at home and mixed so little with other children; on the other hand, they were happy because being so "quiet" made her very easy to look after. The participant said that books and stories had been her all-consuming passion. She had easily become totally immersed in them, spending hours on end absorbed in her books to the point of forgetting everything around her. She felt magically attracted to the world in her books, almost as if she herself were part of the unfolding story. The world around her would then totally disappear, as if she had taken psychedelic drugs. She did however express surprise about the direction of the current constellation, as 30 years had since elapsed, and she found it hard to imagine that this earlier period could still be having an effect in the present. These days she read a lot less and hadn't thought about this period of her childhood and youth for many years.

I asked the representative whether she thought she would be able to turn away from the wall to look at her potential partner. She said she couldn't and told me in a small, childlike voice that there was no way she would be able to take her eyes off the wall: that is, the "screen." I then asked her whether she was feeling like an adult or a child. Like a child, came the reply.

As the representative for the participant was obviously reaching back in time to her childhood self, I asked the participant to set up a second representative for her adult self. She did so, placing the representative for the "adult" immediately next to the "child" so that the two of them were set up along the same axis. The "adult" was however looking to her left, at the child. The two of them stood like this for a long time. The "child" avoided looking at the "adult" and continued

74

to stare at the wall. Then the older "self" said this to the younger one: "Come with me, I need you. We belong together." The younger "self" seemed to be afraid of moving away from the wall, from the safety of the familiar. The older self said, "You can trust me. We'll be happier if we're together. Come, I'll help you." Slowly and cautiously she placed her arm around the shoulders of her younger counterpart and carefully and tenderly moved her away from the wall. The child's legs were still visibly wobbly as she took a look around her. Everything seemed so new to her, as if she were seeing the real world for the first time. The two of them took a few steps. Slow and uncertain steps, but steps all the same. But for both representatives it was too early to look at the potential partner. The older woman said to him, "Give us a little time and we'll come back when we're ready." And this is where we left it.

In retrospect it looks as if the participant had in her youth used reading as a way of withdrawing from the world. She used reading and the stories in her books as a kind of drug to allow her to dream her way into another world. The books let her lose herself in another reality without really seeing it for what it was. She could always take refuge in this other world if she needed to as a way of gaining protection from the harsh world "outside." From the outside, however, it had looked as if she was just reading, and nobody—including her—had noticed just how much she was withdrawing into this world of the imagination. As an adult she moved to another city and there her books—her portal into the world of the imagination—ceased to play such a key role. But there was still unfinished business—to liberate the inner child from the world in which it was still captive and to take it along into their common future. The "potential partner" would just have to wait for a while until the participant was ready to reunite the two parts of herself.

A Father Hangs Himself for His Daughter?

This constellation took place in Hannover. A young woman described her emotional state as extremely unbalanced, oscillating between extremes of aggression and depression. She felt trapped, unable to go forwards. When I asked her if there had been any drastic events in her family system, she told me, among other things, that her father had hanged himself when she was just three years of age. She had resented him for his suicide because she had needed him to be her father, and he hadn't been there. "Actually," as she put it, "he just cleared off." But what she didn't know or, I suspected, understand sufficiently well was this: people don't usually commit suicide arbitrarily or deliberately to harm others. From systemic practice we know that suicides are often entangled in their family system and follow this destiny.

We set up two representatives: the woman herself and her father. The participant placed the two representatives a considerable distance apart, but the representative for the father was able to look at his daughter without the daughter being able to see him in return because she was looking in the opposite direction. It didn't take long for the representative for the father to begin to get upset. He told us that he was feeling very odd and that something was rising up within him. He repeatedly puffed up his cheeks, almost as if a safety valve were letting out large volumes of air. His whole demeanor led me to suspect that something was coming over him that he was unable to control and was proving too much for him. I asked him what was going on inside. He replied that there was something "bad" in him that had taken complete possession of him. It was getting stronger and stronger and had him utterly in its power; it was for all the world as if he were drunk with it. "I'm glad my daughter is standing so far away," he said, "because in this state there's no telling what I might do. I feel like Dracula and Frankenstein's monster all rolled into one—and that's one hell of a murderous mix." He told me that he couldn't possibly inflict his state on anyone else. Others would be better off without him. What he really wanted to do was to get out of the room.

I asked him to stay for a while. I then asked the representative for the participant about her experience. She admitted to being afraid of what was going on behind her back. There was something disturbing going on, and she didn't want to risk turning round. I then suggested to the representative for the father that he use the following sentence—but only if it felt right for him to do so. Quietly but clearly, he said that sentence to his daughter: "I did it for you!" Silence descended. The representative for the daughter slowly turned a little toward the father. I gave the father a few more sentences to say—again with the proviso that they felt right. He carried on: "I left so that you could stay! It was meant as a gift—please take it. Make something out of it and be happy in your life. Please take it as a gift. Don't be angry with me. I give you my blessing for your future." The representative for the daughter now turned fully to face her father. Clearly very moved, she slowly walked up to him, embraced him tenderly and said, "Dad, I can take it from you now." After a while the representative for the father released himself slowly from his daughter's embrace, turned slowly around, went out the door and closed it behind him. At this point I ended the constellation.

A constellation such as this is of course quite a challenge to our rational mind. It's hard to swallow the realization that something like this could happen. But some of the things which happen in the human soul are difficult for reason to comprehend. Those processes of true significance are often completely inaccessible to the rational mind. If we want to find a solution we have to learn to look differently. Complex and opaque processes will then often reveal themselves as clear and easy to understand. In this case, something manifested very clearly: The father seemed to be "drunk" on his murderous energy. He was probably also entangled in his family of origin. What probably happened was that, in order to make sure that he didn't harm anyone (including his own daughter), he decided that the world (and his daughter) was safer without him. From his perspective at that time it was probably the best thing he could do for his daughter. He did it out of love for others. Having had a chance to see things from his point of view, his daughter was now finally able to look back on her father with love, take the gift he had offered, and get on with her life.

Mother Stays so that Daughter Can Stay

The following example is a constellation that I did for a woman in Berlin. She was complaining of feeling ill-at-ease and depressed. Since her mother's death many years previously the symptoms had steadily got worse. She told me that she had known as a child that her mother wanted to die. She had always been ill, sometimes even at death's door: to the point where she had on occasion expressed a desire to die. The daughter had on several occasions found her mother lying unconscious on the floor and called the ambulance, which had helped keep her mother alive. The daughter told me that she felt that her mother had put herself through hell unnecessarily: she could have gone earlier; then she wouldn't have suffered so grievously.

We set up the constellation: a representative for the woman and one for her mother. She placed the representatives so that they were a little distance apart but could see each other. The two women stood there for a while in silence. I then asked the representative for the daughter what was going on for her, and she replied that she was looking at her mother full of pity: "My poor mother put herself through so much torment." I then asked the representative for the mother what she could see. She withdrew into herself for a long time before finally emerging and saying this: "You know what, I'm not a 'poor mother'. I'm at peace with myself. It's not me you have to worry about—it's you. I knew that if I left this world too soon, you would follow soon after. I knew that if I went before you were independent enough to stand on your own two feet, you would follow me. I couldn't go until you were out of danger. I had to wait until you were old enough to be safe. You were more at risk than I was because you didn't know about any of this. It's true that I would have liked to have gone earlier. But I stayed out of love for you so that you wouldn't have to go the same way as me. I wanted you to stay here even after I had gone. And it worked, didn't it? Please take this present from me and make something of it so that I can see that it wasn't all in vain. I did it for you; please accept it as a gift." The representative for the daughter was visibly moved and said, "Thank you. I had no idea that you did everything for me so that I could stay. Now I can take it from you with love. I will honor you by taking this gift and I will make something out of it."

This constellation is pretty self-explanatory. The participant recognized how strong her mother had really been. With a little bit of time, she really would now be able to accept the gift.

A Dog Needs to Be Stroked

This was a constellation for a dog. His owner was having difficulties with him because he was constantly demanding to be stroked. He was much too clingy, and his desire for intimacy and physical affection was too strong for her liking. And even when he got the strokes and attention that he had been after, he still never seemed to be satisfied. She was at her wit's end. We set up the constellation: a representative for the dog and one for the participant.

Both felt their way into their roles. Before long the representative for the dog pointed to an area of floor in front of him that he felt compelled to look at. This spot was attractive and interesting to him and was absorbing all his attention. In the initial interview the participant had among other things admitted to being angry with her mother and to having broken off all contact with her. I now set up a representative for the mother on the spot the dog was looking at. The representative for the dog was immediately relieved. He pointed to the representative for the mother and said, "I want her. She's important to me. It's her I really want to be stroked by!" The representative for the dog then turned to the representative for the participant and said, "That's what you've got to do too. Being stroked by her is great." And this is where we left the constellation.

The issue had become as clear as day: the dog seemed to be wanting to tell his owner that she should again look to her mother to "stroke" her. This meant that he didn't actually want to be stroked himself at all; what he wanted was to move his owner to seek affection from her mother—to take her into her heart and love her. The participant initially found this hard to swallow because she had made her mind up that she was always going to be angry with her mother. But the dog and the constellation had moved her to reconsider her position and let the experience sink in.

Chapter 5

Walking-In-Your-Shoes in Combination with Systemic Elements from Family Constellation

As I've already mentioned, my work with Walking-In-Your-Shoes has over the years proved to be effective. From the processes I can derive insights into the inner world of the people, animals or elements Walked. The classic Walk, in which only person is involved, is often sufficient in itself to set an inner process in motion and lead the participant to a deeper understanding of the situation. Only one Walker is involved in this process; no further elements are added. The advantage of this is that the process can remain clear and be kept relatively short, no longer than 10 to 20 minutes.

Sometimes, however, it can be useful to bring in one or more elements from Family Constellations. This often adds a quality to the Walk and can take things to a still deeper level. This can for instance be brought about by another person. Who that person should be can easily become very clear indeed, for example when the Walker says, "I miss my mother." Then it can make sense to add a further representative and see if the Walk changes. This isn't of course to say that it always makes sense to add a further representative every time the Walker indicates he would like one. At this point the facilitator has to intuit which variant will have the greater effect.

Another example is when the Walker spends the entire Walk looking in one direction. Then it can make sense to set up a representative for whatever he is trying to see in order to derive further insights from the Walk. Either that or it becomes clear that the Walker is trying to avoid a certain part of the room. In this case it can be an option to set up a representative for whatever the Walker is trying to avoid to see if anything changes and what the area of difficulty might be. It's also always possible to release such an element if it doesn't seem to be taking the Walk anywhere. It's better not to cling to a particular idea if it is only yielding poor results. In such a case a more profitable approach would be to try out another element and see if something important has been overlooked or even to start the Walk again from scratch.

I frequently include the participant himself as a further element in the Walk. In other words, I ask the participant to get up and take part in the Walk himself as directed by his own intuition. If, for instance, his own father or mother is being Walked and the process has revealed some important insights and understandings, things can sometimes go even deeper if the participant himself is included in the Walk. The interaction between the two can often provide another way in.

Other elements which can be borrowed from Family Constellations include things like "the future," "happiness" or "love." It's also possible to Walk guilt, a country or a vocation. Depending on the way the Walk pans out, it can make sense to use any one of these. There's no limit to the number of possible new variants. In order to illustrate all this more clearly I have in the following put together a few examples of combined processes.

Roots

A participant told me that she was looking for her roots and felt unable to find her rightful place in life; an experience which was shared by her daughters, she says. She didn't want to select the Walker herself and asked me to do it for her. I chose a man to be the Walker for her roots.

The Walker got up, went to the middle of the room and got ready to begin the Walk. When he was ready, he said, "I am now 'Angelika's roots'" (the name has been changed, like in all examples). To start with, nothing happened. We waited for the first step. The Walker leaned over, almost as if he were trying to get his body moving. It didn't work. He now tried desperately to take the first step, but his body refused to move. He tried again—in vain. There was just too much resistance in his legs. He was also feeling a heavy load on his shoulders which, as he told us, was the worst part of it; it felt as though he were made of concrete. After a while (he still hadn't managed to take a single step), he noticed something behind him. Something was there which felt like a foreign body. I asked him to carry on paying attention to it. All at once a clear image presented itself to him: the foreign body felt like foreign troops occupying his country.

I asked the participant whether anyone from her family of origin was from another country or had been forced to flee their native land. The participant replied that her grandmother had been born in what is now the Czech Republic—the former Czechoslovakia—and that she had fled the country during the Third Reich and left everything behind. The flight sounded truly terrible: her grandma had been forced to travel by road, sometimes even on foot, even though the whole family was of Sudeten German extraction. I now asked the participant to select a person to be the Czech Republic and to use her intuition to place them. She set up "the Czech Republic" at the edge of the room, at some distance from the "roots" As soon as "the Czech Republic" came on the scene we could all see that there was a definite relationship between the two representatives: They looked at each other for a long time.

The Walker for the "roots" looked at "the Czech Republic" and prepared to go over to it. But his progress was very slow and extremely laborious because he couldn't shake off his burden and the feeling of being set in concrete, making the journey appear very arduous. Shaking with exertion and on the verge of exhaustion he made his way step by step toward the "country." It seemed to take forever and to become more arduous with every step, but the Walker finally managed—by the end crawling on all fours—to reach "the Czech Republic." By then, all the Walker for the roots could do in the depths of his exhaustion was to extend a single finger to the "country": happily, the "country" responded by taking his whole hand. This physical contact seemed to do them both a lot of good; it became warmer and more intimate, culminating in a tight embrace. At this point "the Czech Republic" was half on its knees and the Walker semi-prone on the floor. The embrace continued to develop until the "roots" (probably representing the grandmother) were lying in the lap of "the Czech Republic" like a child. Everything was now fine. "The Czech Republic" stroked the Walker for the roots tenderly, and the "roots" were feeling protected and secure. The Walker for the roots said, "I'm there. At last!"

The following picture emerged from the period of reflection with the other participants: the grandmother's roots seemed to be desperately homesick for their native soil and wanted to go back home, to the Czech Republic, or Czechoslovakia as it used to be. And this was exactly what the participant was connected with deep down, without even knowing it. Her inner narrative seemed to be something like this: "If I dispense with my roots as well, my darling grandmother, I will feel close to you." It seems highly probable that the grandmother still had an immense longing for the country which she had been forced to leave in such painful circumstances. Perhaps it was just as hard for the grandmother as it was for the Walker when he was trying to get to the representative for Czechoslovakia. The Walk finished with a significant symbolic act: "the country" was prepared to take "the grandmother" back into its bosom—just as a mother would take her child into her lap to protect it. The "child" could now be back at home with the "mother."

For the participant it was important to see what appeared to be the grandmother's unfinished business—this would empower her to stop carrying the longing and sense of rootlessness around with her but instead to leave both of them where they belonged: with her grandmother.

The Wall of Silence

The following example was taken from a workshop in Hannover. A woman was keen to have her relationship with other members of her family Walked. She told us that a sister, two uncles and two aunts were still living but she was out of contact with them. Why that was, she didn't exactly know. She selected a Walker, who prepared herself for the Walk and then set off.

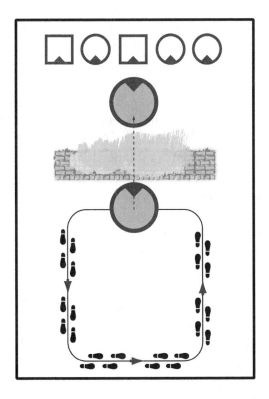

The Walker started Walking in small circles round the room. She told us that everything felt familiar to her: okay but boring. Nothing much was happening; she didn't even really want to talk, because it wouldn't make any difference what she said. As she was speaking it became apparent that she was only using about half the room. She wasn't setting foot in the other half at all. I asked her why she was avoiding the other half, and her reply was that this other area felt a bit creepy. Something over there was making her feel uneasy, which was why she preferred to stay in her own half. I then asked her what she thought might be making her uneasy, but she couldn't say. I now asked her to approach the other side to find out what might be lurking there. She approached the middle of the room—the point at which the other side began—very slowly and cautiously. She was a bit scared but also excited. Moving ever more slowly and with increasing caution, she plucked up the courage to actually approach the border. The closer she got, she reported, the foggier it was getting all around her. Now she had finally reached the border, which felt like a wall, completely surrounded by dense mist. I asked her to take a deliberate step to get to the other side. Her reply was, however, that she wouldn't be able to do it alone; she would need a "push" to get moving. I asked if I might be able to give her the "push" myself. She assented but told me that she would have to go in backwards. I placed my hands on her shoulders, checked to see if she was ready and, when she gave the word, I gave her a vigorous but not overly forceful push backwards onto the other side.

She was now standing right in the middle of the other part of the room. She looked around and tried to get a sense of what had changed. For a while she pirouetted around like a dancer. As she told us, everything on this side was utterly new for her. Here she had a sense of "fullness"; here she felt very widely connected. Everything was completely different from anything she had ever known, and she had no idea why she had avoided this side. Here she felt empowered, and speaking was once again beginning to feel meaningful and enjoyable. It really did look as if this was the case.

I now took the five representatives for the living relatives from her family system to form a constellation on this side, so that all of them were ranged in front of the Walker. She said this: "Yes, that's it. These are the people I was looking for. I feel connected with them now on this side. I'm glad you're here. I now take you as my relatives, and you can have me as your relative." At this point I ended the Walk.

We sat down with the participant and wondered whether there might have been a foggy "wall of silence" between the two sides of the room. If so, we had in this Walk also seen some indications of how it might be taken down.

Aborted Child

A woman in Berlin wanted to have her grown-up daughter Walked. She told me that her daughter wasn't really feeling all of her strength and could be developing more positively than she currently was. The mother was hoping to gain some insight into how she might be able to give her daughter some inner support. She selected a woman to do the Walk for her daughter.

The Walker began the Walk. Before she had even managed a complete lap of the room she was suddenly overwhelmed by panic. She left the circle by the shortest possible route and lay down on a little mattress lying around in the room. She cried, screamed and appeared thoroughly desperate. She wanted a blanket to cover herself up with. I laid a blanket over her. Once she was under the blanket she calmed down a little but continued to shiver and sob. She told me that she felt very small, like a baby, and needed the blanket to protect her. At the same time she said that it was much too bright in the room and she had to protect herself from the light. Things were better in the dark, which was why she wanted to hide herself away.

I asked the mother what might be meant by the reference to "the baby." Her reply was that she had many years previously had an abortion. The mother was sure that something had been "wrong" with the abortion but didn't want to talk about it other than to say that she had no doubt this was what her daughter was feeling. I then asked the mother to stand up and go to the Walker for her daughter. The mother gave an impression of concentrated resolve, as if she knew what she had to do. I let her do what she considered to be right. The mother went over to her daughter and sat down on the floor next to the little bundle that was her daughter's Walker. She gently touched the Walker's head, and the shaking began to abate. The mother said, "You sensed what happened to me and the child. Yes, I tried to repress it, but something was unresolved. I'm now going to take responsibility for it. You don't need to do anything more. Leave it with me. I'll take care of it. At this point the blanket opened, the Walker for the daughter broke into a smile, and they hugged each other tightly.

Vocation

In Berlin, a participant in one of my Walking-In-Your-Shoes trainings wanted to have her vocation Walked. She told me she felt she was out of her depth and unsure of herself. We were both hoping that the Walk would give us some answers. The participant selected a Walker for her vocation. The Walker began as always by saying the sentence: "I am now ' ...'s vocation'."

She began to Walk in circles. She let her shoulders relax, and what struck me was how strong and powerful her gait was. Whilst she was Walking she would frequently make eye contact with the other participants sitting around her in a circle and smile at them. The circles gradually became bigger and bigger, bringing her ever closer to the circle of chairs. She looked full of energy and alert. She made a point of looking every other participant in the eye, as if she were scrutinizing them, and appeared to enjoy it. She said this to them: "You are all my clients. I can help you. You and you and you and you ... I can help you," all the while looking every single one of them in the eye. Everyone felt as if they were being personally addressed, so there was naturally enough a good deal of amusement amongst the observers. The Walker, however, would not be distracted and continued to project an attitude that was both relaxed and serious whilst carrying on in the same vein: "I can work with all of you. With you, with you, with you ..."

I then introduced another representative into the Walk as a "client" of hers. I asked him to find his own place, and he placed himself in a neutral spot, neither at the periphery nor right in the middle of the room. The Walker now started to relate to her client. Initially she just scrutinized him for a while before placing herself almost directly in front of him and saying, "Yes, I can help you too." At which point the client, somewhat skeptical, said, "Go on then ..." So she now approached him and touched his shoulder. He turned away slightly from her. When she neared him again, he said, "No, no, you're doing it all wrong! Do you know what—I'm placing my greatest cares, my biggest problem and all my vulnerability completely in your hands. If I'm to get better, I need your help in a way that's good for me. Let me show you how you can help me." He asked her to stand behind him. The Walker for the vocation indicated without speaking that she was ready to learn. She placed herself behind the client as asked. He felt carefully behind him, took her hands and laid them on his forehead. Then he told her that he felt much better because he could now feel how she was helping him. He became a little sad, and you could see how he was entering more fully into his "process." After a while the client got a sense of which was the best position for him. He asked her to sit cross-legged on the floor. This she was happy to do. Then the client lay down on the floor on his back with his head in her lap. He asked her again to place her hands on his forehead. We were now able to see how the representative for the client was getting ever more deeply into his process and his healing. And this was the right way.

The Walker for the vocation was also happy because she now knew what she had learnt: if you want to help, you have to do it in a way that the person seeking help can accept. And you have to know how to do this. Otherwise your attempt to help will be in vain.

The participant in my training was happy and grateful to be able to take this insight home with her.

Unfinished Business with Father

This Walk took place in Hannover. A male participant was particularly interested in looking at his father in a Walk. He told us that his father was very old and had for quite a while been ill and tired. The participants question was whether there might be some unfinished business for his father, and whether something might be preventing him from going.

He selected the Walker for his father. As the Walker set off, however, he seemed to be making heavy weather of it. His legs seemed weak and tired, and he could barely drag himself to the window. Having finally reached the window, he stopped and looked out. He stood there for a long time. He then expressed a desire to leave, telling us that he would rather be elsewhere. But it was clear that something wasn't right: there was obviously some unfinished business. There was still something that he was waiting for.

So at this point I selected a representative for whatever the father's unfinished business was. I asked him to find his own place, and he placed himself in the center of the room so that he was looking at the father, who was himself still looking out of the window. Nothing happened for quite a while; then the Walker for the father silently turned around and looked at the representative for the "unfinished business." He slowly approached the "unfinished business" until he was standing right in front of it. The representative for the unfinished business knelt down and said to the father, "Please look at me. Please look at me now. The time is now." As the father spoke, a depth of emotion was apparent in his voice when he said: "It's good that you're here. Now I can see you."

I asked the participant what effect this was having on him. His reply was that he could see himself in the other representative for the "unfinished business" and was feeling a strong impulse to go and take his place. I gave my consent to this, releasing the representative for the "unfinished business" and having the participant himself take his place. The Walker for the father laid his hand on the head of his son and said this: "I'm sorry if I never really noticed you. There was so much in the way. Now I can see you as you are. It's good that you're here now." The son was very moved. He thanked his father and stood up. The two then embraced warmly. After a while, the Walker for the father slowly turned round without a word and went back to the window. He told us that the unfinished business had been resolved for him and everything was okay. And this is where we left it.

A week later the participant sent me an e-mail telling me that his father had peacefully died in his sleep. And he himself was now also at peace.

Manager and Employee

A woman in Berlin wanted to have her manager Walked. She told us that we she wasn't sure if she should keep her job under him, because there was always so much tension between them. This was causing her a lot of difficulty, and her work was also suffering. She was hoping that the Walk could give her an indication of which decision would be the right one. She selected a Walker for her boss, and he began to Walk. He said, "I am now your boss."

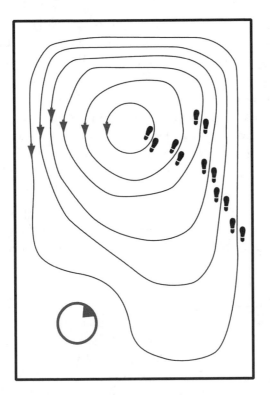

The Walker started to Walk round the room in circles. But after a while he began to hesitate. He became increasingly ruminative, stopping in his tracks and then starting again. He even placed a hand on his forehead, indicating a really strenuous thought process. The impression he gave was that of an absent-minded professor. This went on for quite a while. He told us that there was something going on inside him that he couldn't grasp. Something was preoccupying and bothering him. At the times when he was "digging around" inside he was completely self-preoccupied, and everything else around him seemed merely to be disturbing his concentration. However, he continued his erratic Walk, sometimes stopping and starting again and repeating the pattern.

I now introduced the participant herself into the Walk; she found her own place, positioning herself at the edge of the inner circle of chairs. The Walker for her boss continued his laps of the room but left out the part of the room in which she was standing, with the effect of creating an "Indentation" in his Walk. This indentation gradually became bigger and bigger, progressively squeezing him and his laps into an even smaller space. He became increasingly agitated, telling us that the other person was making him feel very constricted and constrained. He even started to get slightly panicky because the space available to him was dwindling so fast. And so it went on.

I asked the participant for her impression. She told me that she had once been in a relationship with her boss which had since ended. On hearing this, I took the participant out of the Walk again and asked her to take a seat. Her boss let out a sigh of relief and began again to use the entire room for his Walk, at which point the dent promptly disappeared. It was actually a lot worse than it looked, he told us, and he was only now beginning to realize just how much pressure he had been under. Repeatedly stressing how great his relief was, he exhaled deeply a couple of times as if releasing further stress and started to look almost cheerful. His Walk ceased to be jerky and became even and relaxed. He started to swing his arms as he Walked, and a contented smile spread over his face. At this point I ended the Walk.

Armed with the information from this Walk, I have no doubt that the participant found it easy to make a decision. Her boss was evidently experiencing a great deal of pressure from having to work with her as an employee. This could have made the participant's professional life very difficult indeed. I suspect that her boss was feeling so conflicted because their private and professional lives had become intertwined with a blurring of the distinction between levels of hierarchy: As a couple they had been on the same level; as manager and employee, however, they had not.

Tiger's Cage

A female participant wanted to examine her ability to sustain relationships and decided to have herself Walked. I agreed, and she selected a woman to do the Walk for her. The Walk began.

After a while we could see that the circular orbit which the Walker was describing was tending to become ever more rectangular in form. She told us that this was the only path she could follow. It looked from the outside as if she were following the course of walls or boundaries. There was something cat-like about her gait, and so I asked her if she were in a cage, for example a tiger's cage. She thought briefly and then said, "Yes, it's true. That's exactly how it is. Absolutely right."

I asked her then to take a very good look and to find her bearings. Then I asked her how she was. Her reply was this: "I could Walk around and around the cage like this for ever. But it makes me feel lonely." I asked her if she could also see the bars of the cage, and she said she could. Then I asked her if she had ever touched the bars, but she hadn't. At this point I asked her to do so, and her reluctance was obvious. She withdrew into herself for a long time before saying in a quiet and calm voice, "I'm not allowed to touch the bars. If I touch them I might discover that they aren't made of iron." The rest of us exchanged astonished glances, and I didn't immediately know what my next question should be. I then tried this: "What do you mean when you say that the bars might not be made of iron?" Her reply was this: "If I touch the bars I might discover that they aren't as strong as they look; I might even be able to bend them apart with my hands because they aren't made of iron." I asked the Walker, "Does that mean that you might be able to bend the bars far enough to get out of the cage?" She hesitated again and seemed to look within for an answer. She then said, "Absolutely. But if I can get out, that also means that somebody could get in!"

Understanding slowly dawned on me. She was staying in the cage to prevent herself from getting out and others from getting in! Our inner being, our soul, can sometimes be simply ingenious. I tried again, introducing another representative into the Walk, someone undefined who was "out there," outside the cage. I set him up a short distance away from the cage.

The two representatives looked at each other. After a while, the Walker's face started to brighten. She told us that she actually quite liked the look of the other person, a sentiment that was immediately echoed by the other. I asked her if she still wanted to remain in the cage or whether she might now want to bend the bars apart and escape. She had now found the strength and the courage to do this and physically took the decisive step of leaving the cage. "It'll take some getting used to out here," she said, "but it's good." She then looked affectionately at the other person and said to him, "I'm here now! And I'm ready!" Upon which the other representative replied, "I'm ready too. We're both ready!"

This Walk was pretty self-explanatory. Afterward I understood why the participant had wanted to start with her ability to be in relationships. There was a two-way process: she would get out of the cage by being prepared to let someone else in. Then she would be free to be in a partner relationship with someone.

Asperger's Syndrome no. 2?

The following example is taken from a workshop I recently held in Hannover. A young man told me that he was suffering from a serious lack of sexual drive and that he found it difficult to approach and talk to women. In fact, his inhibition was so pronounced that he couldn't even imagine doing so, although he wasn't attracted to men. We discussed which might be a suitable role and decided on his "self-esteem." So I asked him to select a Walker. For this role he selected a woman.

The Walker began to Walk around but appeared unsure as to how and where she should Walk. She then tried out various areas of the room, starting off in the brighter part of the room close to the window before crossing to the darker part on the other side. She seemed unable to make up her mind about which part of the room to be in. It was lighter at the window but also more exciting—and more dangerous. On the opposite side it was darker but also more boring and safer. She told us that something important was missing but was unable to say what it was. Finally she ended up back at the window. She looked out of it for a long time, with her gaze cast up toward the sky. She then said that she would really rather be somewhere else. She had been wondering the whole time whether she should just leave the room. She carried on looking at the sky and told us that that was where she wanted to be. The sky, a place "way out there," was offering her a promise of fulfillment—here in the room she was in the wrong place; everything was too cramped.

I then introduced another representative for whatever it was that was "way out there." This latter, also a woman, went and stood very close to the Walker for "self-esteem," who didn't show any inclination to relate to her, continuing instead to look through the window up into the sky. At this point I released the other representative, and she sat down. However, something seemed now to be moving for the self-esteem Walker. She now asked herself out loud: "How would it be if I stopped looking all the way up to the sky for my happiness but could instead find it right here on earth?" This new question really seemed to inspire her, and she turned away from the window. "What a fantastic idea! It just hadn't occurred to me! Wouldn't it be great if I could find my happiness right here where I am!"

She reoriented herself physically in the room and started looking around to see how and where she might find her happiness. But now another difficulty presented itself. Now she was finding the sheer number of people in the room intimidating. She reported feeling that everyone was looking at her, and this was preventing her from finding her own way. She ended up looking at the floor. I asked all the participants in the room to look away for a while so that we would be able to see how things might develop with the self-esteem. Everyone obliged by either looking away or covering their eyes. I told the participant that the "coast was now clear" and she could look up. She did so, and things now started to get easier for her. She found that she could now get her bearings. At the same time she noticed how new everything was and that nothing was familiar. She was seeing everything for the first time! But she couldn't shake the feeling that something significant was missing. There was something she didn't know—she told us that she didn't understand the situation. I asked the Walker what she meant. She in turn asked me to explain the situation to her. Without knowing exactly what she meant by that, I had a go by telling her this: "We're doing a Walk here, and you are a Walker." But this wasn't the explanation she'd been looking for, and she felt none the wiser. She then said, "What I really need is someone to explain the world to me. I don't understand the world! That's what's missing! I really wish I had someone to explain to me what's going on. I don't get what's happening. And I don't understand people. I just can't read them."

I introduced a representative for a "friend and helper" into the Walk. He linked arms with "self-esteem," and they Walked together for a while. The Walker for self-esteem asked the friend to explain the situation to her, and this is what he said: "Okay, so you're confused and uncertain right now, but that doesn't matter. If you want to know anything, just ask me. Look, other people like you. They're looking away because they want to help you." Happy and relieved, the self-esteem Walker said that this was exactly the help she needed. "Actually," she added, "If I don't understand something I can ask people myself. It's nice to have a friend at my side, but I can ask for myself!" The self-esteem appeared to have been reinforced and to have some new impetus. And this is where we left it.

So what had the Walk revealed? My view of things was that the young man had not believed that he would be able to find happiness in a world that he didn't understand. He might secretly have believed he that happiness and self-esteem were to be found "somewhere out

96

there"—somewhere he felt he could cope better than here. At any rate, it wasn't working where he was now. And when the Walk first offered the opportunity to look closer to home, he established just how difficult it really was for him. But he was able to develop coping strategies to find a way to understand the world and other people. The participant himself found that the Walk had given him a great deal of encouragement and positive impetus for the future.

Again, what was revealed here was somewhat akin to the inner world of a person with Asperger's syndrome.

Further Reflections and Thoughts

Why Does Being Walked Work?
Or Rediscovering Mysticism

Many people have devoted themselves to finding out how and why a Constellation or Walk of an issue by one or more representatives actually works. Whole books have been written on the subject. What seems to come into play to such effect in these contexts is referred to by the literature as the "knowing field" or "morphogenetic field." The assumption is that information which is somehow stored becomes visible and identifiable in particular situations, such as the constellations or Walks described in this book. I myself sometimes use the term "cloud of information" to describe the environment the representatives find themselves in when they are taken over by a role. However, no one has ever yet delivered a conclusive, comprehensible or plausible explanation of why the representatives feel and perceive what they do. This is why I have taken the decision to leave to all attempts to explain this phenomenon to those people who are actually interested in finding out. I am personally totally unconcerned about seeking answers and am instead happy to accept that there are some things which can't be explained. But it somehow still amuses me to see how many people carry on trying to find answers, even though I think they are barking up completely the wrong tree. After all, the enormous challenge this poses to our rational mind and cognitive faculty means that aiming to integrate newly-discovered phenomena into old structures and perspectives is completely fruitless; instead, we have no choice but to attempt to discover new structures and perspectives which transcend the old.

It's my opinion that we are in actual fact only just beginning to address the issue of whether our scientific-technological world-view might need to give way to a descriptive mysticism. The fact is that increasing numbers of people are using alternative and complementary methods such as acupuncture, homeopathy, Family Constellations, Walking, Bach flower remedies, yoga and meditation. At the same time, many are turning their backs on expensive and relatively ineffective, purely scientific methods (including conventional medicine). I have had participants in my workshops who have undergone twenty years of psychotherapy without making any discernible progress whatsoever. After a Family Constellation, however, they have reported making progress in leaps and bounds in comparison to their psychotherapeutic treatment.

At the same time, there's no getting away from the fact that, without Freud, without psychotherapy, without psycho- and linguistic analysis, without the other important successors to Freud and discoverers of the "soul," we would not have got to where we are today. What we have today is the consequence of a development, a further link in the same chain. We've now got to the point where we may perhaps be forced to acknowledge that our newly acquired insights could change our whole modern world view. We will have to wait and see what shape this process takes.

If you yourself have ever been a representative in a constellation or a Walker in a Walk, it may be that you too have sensed the role of another person. What I wonder is this: Do you really want to find rational explanations for this phenomenon or are you just unwilling to subject your old world view to scrutiny?

At the end of the day, our modern, "enlightened" scientific worldview arose out of a rejection of mysticism. People were tired of wandering about in helpless thrall to the arbitrary workings of a kind of vague mysticism. Instead of inchoate and vague mystery, they wanted to create clear structures. In old Europe, people were no longer prepared to believe that everything could be right and wrong at one and the same time. They no longer wanted to be subject to this impenetrable thicket of possibilities. They wanted structures, perspective, regularity and order. Nor did they want to be in thrall to God; instead they created science. Everything then seemed much clearer; people found they could see with much greater clarity. The darkness of mysticism gave way to the bright light of science. Enthusiasm abounded—until today, that is.

In our era, confronted with the progressive destruction of the environment and global warming, we have to ask whether this path is the right one for us or whether we shouldn't place our faith in something new: the "re-mystification" and "deceleration" of our world. We can't explain everything. As humans, our rational faculty isn't quite as strong as we like to think. Okay, so our strength of inner perception has lagged behind our scientific development. But now, in tandem with the rediscovery of mysticism, we have an opportunity to revive the faculty that we buried way back when.

In this connection I would like briefly to state my position on a further point which might give us an idea of how those issues which we have lost sight of or consciously or unconsciously rejected or simply disregarded manifest in our society. In my daily practice with certain social groups I often perceive a deeper systemic-societal function of their problems and issues: a function which reminds us systemically of what we have shut out or forgotten. Things which are repressed and pushed away on a social and individual basis come to light elsewhere. So, for instance, I wonder whether the hippy generation was trying to remind us that we had repressed and rejected mysticism and "unreason." The "return of the repressed" might herald the emergence of a new perspective to infuse the world afresh with the magic of which it has been stripped.

The Soul, or What Really Happens

By way of explanation of why the use of representatives in Walking-In-Your-Shoes and Family Constellations works and what really happens in the process, we can draw on the concept of "movements of the soul."

The word "soul" is very commonly used: in philosophy, religion and therapy and in everyday life. The sheer elusiveness of the soul and its unwillingness to subject itself to the scrutiny of the inquiring mind has been a source of dispute and frustration amongst philosophers since time immemorial. Some philosophers have found this such an intractable problem that their response has been to ditch the soul altogether. However, other more open-minded thinkers have been unwilling to be accused of disregarding and ignoring something that self-evidently exists and have for a range of motives devoted themselves to exploring this issue. It might appear stupid but the fact of the matter is that we have something here whose existence we can't simply discount, even if it cannot be explained by biology, medicine, psychology, genetic research, chemistry or any other scientific discipline! However tempted one might be to simply let it lie, the "soul" refuses to go away.

The word is also frequently used in daily life. We might for example say "the poor soul" or talk about doing something with "heart and soul." But neither philosophers nor non-philosophers can actually explain exactly what is meant by it. Not all that long ago, a mere two or three centuries back, a common view was that the soul was located in particular parts of the body. Or did it actually belong to God—or even the devil?

From a modern-day perspective these thoughts seem pretty far out, but what they do show is how helpless and fumbling we are in our dealings with the concept of the soul. The difficulty is this: It exists, and yet it doesn't exist.

Seen in a particular light, of course it doesn't exist. In other words, the soul cannot be found in a particular place. We can't put our finger on it and isolate it like a liver or kidney. And it's also difficult to convey to others what a "soul" actually is. Seen from another perspective, it's obvious that the soul does exist. How else could we possibly describe the deepest processes in our inner world? How else could we express the uniqueness of our experience and the mechanics of our individual "universe"? What other idea could we use to give expression to the place we need to look for the confusion and wrong-headedness that makes our life so difficult and, in some cases, even impossible?

At this point, our all-powerful rationality loses its significance. Because, notwithstanding all the insights it delivers, the true essence of the human being will always elude it because of its inability to operate outside categories and disciplines. As far as biology is concerned, for example, there is too little chlorophyll, bone or chromosome in the soul for it to be identified. For chemistry, there's too little reference to periodic table, litmus or carbon. And there's too little of the stuff of x-ray, injection and transplantation to make it accessible to medicine. As far as genetic research is concerned, it's no good because you can't isolate it in a test tube, nor is it sufficiently modern and innovative. For psychology (or at least elements thereof), it isn't accessible to statistical analysis; there's too little predictability and visibility.

So let's just leave these categories to one side and stop worrying about definitions within a rational system. The soul isn't rational: it's much greater than that. And what's more, it wants something from us! It requires nothing less than our surrender: without stint, without concealing ourselves behind a wall of hypocrisy and sanctimony. As Nietzsche put it: "What is clear and what is clarified through explanation?" If we could just let go of the need to explain things, perhaps they would become clear.

As a philosophy student, certain rational comments never failed to get my hackles up, for example: "What, you want to be a philosopher? Then you'll no doubt be able to explain to me the meaning of life." These days, when confronted with this kind of view, I just say tongue in cheek: "If you want to know the meaning of life, go and find a therapist ..."

The soul manifests. In all the examples described in this book it becomes visible as that which otherwise lurks behind the difficulties. It is what we are. The concept of "soul" is merely a code, a cipher. Anyone who has submitted a box number advertisement to a newspaper knows how this works. The box number itself has no meaning. Its only purpose is to bring client and customer together. Do you get my drift? The word "soul" is merely a cipher for something behind it. And the "something" behind it manifests through its effect. This effect is visible, identifiable and tangible! How could we otherwise explain "conscience" without soul; what about "shame" or "morality" or even "depression"? We can recognize the soul by its effect and by the "flowers" that emerge everywhere from its "bud." Just look at the flowers brought forth by the participants in the above examples. We can join together and look at all the flowers that emerge like a beautiful garden and say: "So that's what it looks like. Incredible!"

When we look so closely and in such depth at this garden we might ask ourselves the question: "What really happens?" And where in this garden is there a place for my flower? And, at the end of the day, isn't this garden the only thing we really have?

Interview with Joseph Culp,
Co-Founder of Walking-In-Your-Shoes

This is a transcribed interview from my audio recordings which was held in March 2009 on two different days. The questions have been chosen by the author.

Interview part 1, on March 20th 2009 in Studio City, California

Christian Assel: Who was involved at the beginning, how did it start and who is involved now?

Joseph Culp: Okay? The beginning of what? The beginning of the Universe? (laughs) What are you asking here exactly? Do you mean, who was involved at the beginning of Walking-In-Your-Shoes and who is involved in it now?

At the very beginning there were two. There were two people involved: myself and John Cogswell. John Cogswell was a Psychotherapist, a Ph.D., who practiced here in southern California for like 30 years or so. He also had an extensive background in Psychology, he had been the head administrator of a mental hospital at one point, anyway, he was in private practice, and it was around 1986 when we were working together. He made a suggestion to me, and the suggestion was based on an exercise that he had once done, actually many, many years before, in an acting class. So it's really interesting how it kind of came full circle to me. The exercise was really to just stimulate me, he was not an actor, he just took it sort of as an amateur to see what it would do to him. It was I think the mid-sixties and he was just expanding his consciousness, and someone had suggested "Walking" as something, I forgot what it was for him, a character perhaps, and without doing very much, just by making a commitment to an intention, he felt sensations and a shift in his awareness, and as a Psychologist he thought that was very interesting that such a minimal application of intention would shift his consciousness in some way: point of view, how he felt … He never really did anything with it, but he always thought it was kind of remarkable. It was a very personal experience for him.

And here we are, it was many years later in 1986, working together, and I who was his client was working on a role for a film that I was going to do, and he made the suggestion that I try Walking the character. And in a way it was an outgrowth of a lot of his own technique in therapy, which had to do with people becoming more aware of their bodies and what was happening energetically in their body and how to give voice to those feelings or energies in their body. I think he had done a lot of bio-energetic work, which is a type of work that releases information from the energy stored in the body. So in a way, him suggesting that was an outgrowth of this own Philosophy, but as a process this was not his practice at all. He had not systematized anything or even said: this is something I know how to do. He just made a suggestion. And what happened is, because of some of my training and some of my willingness, I said sure, I'll try that, try Walking as a character. But I won't try imitating anything, I won't try making it up.

And that was the big difference. It wasn't me doing an improvisation, saying: "Now here is the character!" and presenting it. It was me just taking the suggestion and then moving without thinking and see if anything happens. And I had a really profound first Walk if you will, it was very much in line or empathizing with this character. I had visions of what it was like as a child, his parents, his sort of relationship to the world and how he saw things … the character was a priest actually, a young novice priest, and I identified with where my power was or what I wanted to do in life. And all these things happened very spontaneously and they felt very personal. It was a personal experience of this character, and I was really amazed by it, and I sat down afterward and—after Walking for 20 minutes or so—I said that was really remarkable! I had been trained in lots of other acting techniques but I never really tried just jumping off like that and just assuming that somehow something will happen. And he was impressed also, and said, you know I have been thinking about this for a while: What is our capacity to empathize with each other, with a character or an idea and where does it translate into our bodies. Why don't we study this a little bit.

So in 1987, about a year later, we formed the first group to study the effects of using this idea. We still hadn't called it "Walking," that didn't come for a while, we called it Walking, because we knew that this was required. But we also knew that Walking wasn't meant literal in the physical sense. It's about a commitment and then starting to notice and put your attention on your body and find out what's happening.

So the first group was with some friends of mine, and we were actors. I said: "Let's go to work with this guy!" and see what happens.

So John Cogswell was learning about what the implications were and we were willing to try, because we were trained to do that, to try things. We worked together for a while in 1987 for a few months and saw some really outstanding things happen. We tried Walking each other. That was really the first thing, because he wanted to know what value would this have in therapy.

We seemed to spontaneously manifest some of the essential qualities or themes of the people that we Walked—and we were confirmed by the people that we Walked, who said: "I don't know how you could do that." How could you understand that little part of me. It's almost like I was Walking there with you. So this connection, this empathic response seemed to be very much real and very natural. But it requires concentration, it requires putting your mind on it.

So that was the beginning. It was John and I and eventually a group of a few other people who tried it out, and then John and I continued to discuss it and tried it in sessions. Then he started to experiment with his clients. He had their permission to Walk them. And this was huge, you know, for him to take that risk, because there is a lot of "opinions" about what is the proper way to work with a client. He often broke some of those rules, nothing terrible, but I mean he went outside the box a bit.

But his clients thought it had a lot of meaning for them. The therapist was getting up and moving as them and they felt very embraced by that. So that part of the therapy was strong for them. These ideas kept surfacing over and over about people feel like they are getting empowered by the Walking. They feel that we're not judging them, we're just embracing them at their very core.

CA: Do you agree that no one knows the answer, no one knows YOUR answer? We'd have to let the "field" know the answer?

Joseph: I think that's a good way to put it, because we never claimed and the Walker certainly doesn't claim to have an answer; they don't even know what they're doing! We just have to move and listen and feel what we feel and report the best we can. So it is like the "field" is working or some kind of larger intelligence is at work there that we can't own per se.

To go ahead with your initial question: Over the next few years we were studying it off and on, and by 1990 we formed a formal study group which was comprised of myself, my now wife, we were just living together at the time, we were both actors plus three other therapists, and a dancer. We did this for over a year, meeting for regular sessions. We would Walk each other, we would Walk clients, we would Walk the people we were working with that weren't present in the room, and parents. We tried all different applications of where it could go, made a lot of notes. This was the first and foremost thing.

And after that, I'd say, over the next 10 years, there were different "incarnations" of groups that John and I would lead. At one point there was more detailed study, I started doing a lot of writing myself, I started the theater group in 1992, where I said I want to work more specifically with actors, writers and directors about using the Walking to help their creativity. John expanded much more in having a full therapist group. That was about a decade of work there.

John semi-retired now, but I know he continues to use the work with the clients that he sees. One of the people that came to work with me, eventually, she started out as an actress learning the Walking. That in some ways was the springboard for her to go into the field of Psychology, and she ended up getting a degree, and by now she's a quite well known therapist here in L.A. who works specifically with sex addicts, sex addiction. She lead a Walking group for a number of years and has applied it directly to the problems of sex addiction, her name is Alex Katehakis. She just published an article where the Walking is mentioned, but it's not about the Walking, it's about part of her work.

So I'm still using it and teaching it in the theater context, in creativity, John in using it, Alex and my wife Lauren are using it. There is another woman named Eugenia, who also first came to work with me as a performer, she became a part of one of the Walking study groups for a while—and eventually she moved back east. She actually renamed the Walking for herself with groups that she would lead in Woodstock, and she called it "Inner Walking," which is sort of a derivation of it, she is still working with it. Now that was a long answer!

CA: Did you say that you first got to know John Cogswell as a client of his?

Joseph: Yes, I was his client.

CA: What exactly is Walking-In-Your-Shoes?

Joseph: So, Walking-In-Your-Shoes has been defined as a body-mind process or a body-mind technique for knowing and being others. That's a very broad kind of term, but it does kind of sum it up: A body-mind technique for knowing and being others.

CA: Can you also know and be "elements"?

Joseph: The truth is, you can apply the knowing and being part to: elements, conditions, concepts if you will. There isn't anything that you can't really apply the Walking to, I think. I remember there was an argument at times about whether you could Walk yourself, and I always thought this was a little bit redundant. It's like, well when you are Walking, in a sense, it is yourself, it's a large part of yourself that's being Walked.

But it was a good point, because you know, I don't want to Walk something else or someone else, I want to Walk me. That has to be honored, and as long as you use the process, if you will, it will apply to you, to any part of yourself that you want to access. But I suppose that notion, you're Walking something that maybe doesn't feel immediate to you, that's why we say "the other" or "others," so it's something that you are distinguishing is separate from you, and in a way the Walking gives you the bridge, gives you the access. So, you are free to Walk yourself, or as people like to Walk their "higher self," this is a very beneficial thing.

It's about "knowing" and "being," the "being," we should underline that, because that's really a type of knowing. In fact, on the Walking-In-Your-Shoes website it says: "A *new* way of knowing." It may not be truly new, but it's new in that application.

A lot of people have come to workshops over the years and talked about that their orientation is too intellectual, it comes from our head. Often that's one of the first steps in training someone in the Walking, I say I really want you to not think about this and not imagine things. Don't think, oh, I have to Walk a bunny rabbit, so what would bunny rabbit look like. We don't want you to do that. I want you to just own it and say that you are the "bunny rabbit" and go ahead. And now start just listen and just feel what happens, so that you are really using being, you don't have to do anything initially.

The benefits that come out of Walking, I think, have to do with that expanded sense of *being*. I am not coming from an intellectual understanding, I am not coming from Jo's or Chris' understanding, I'm just going in to being and seeing what I get there. The Walking is a way to facilitate that. So it's way of knowing and *being*.

CA: What is the origin of the phrase "Walking-In-Your-Shoes"?

Joseph: What we found was, we were calling this: "The Walking," because it would require ourselves to get up and move, and movement was required because it facilitated, again, a type of energetic learning, an energetic movement, where motion reveals something in our field. When we use our bodies and we go in motion, energy is released. In the Walking process that energy often is information. It's emotional information, it's physical information, and if you explore it or stay with that particular motion, something comes up, and the energy that comes up will turn into information and that information can tell you a lot.

It can tell you a lot about the person you are Walking and maybe how to move further with that person. So, motion was important, Walking was important, and we were still just calling it "the Walking."

But there was an other element here, a type of empathy, a type of spontaneous, physical, moving empathy, and there is the old expression, a Native American expression, that you can never know a man until you Walked a mile in his Moccasins.

Now that is a Philosophy that many people have agreed with, over the years. You can look at someone, you can sympathize with them, you can have thoughts about them, but you will never know what that person's life is about until you are able to mentally somehow get "into their skin," you know, Walk a Mile in his Moccasins, Walk a mile in their shoes. Well that's where it came from, and we're doing that, and we're kind of almost doing it literally. We're getting up and saying: "I am now going to be "this person," start Walking around and regard everything that happens as that person. I am going to have an experience and I am willing to risk dropping my own ego, temporarily, and be them. That's what that Philosophy really means. It means: stop coming from who you think you are and allow yourself to enter that person, that world.

So, that's a long way of saying, it was using the old Native American wisdom and that phrase. I don't know if there is a specific tribe it came from, but it has been around for a long time.

So we called it Walking in YOUR shoes, not OUR shoes, THEIR shoes, being willing to step out of ourselves and Walking in YOUR shoes.

CA: I guess the medicine men also used the Walking. They Walked their ancestors, didn't they?

Joseph: You are right. A big part of the Native American culture was shaman work. Medicine men would do Walks or vision quests where you go out and you do Walk; you Walk sometimes for days ... then you come back and you have an experience, and you'll know how to heal somebody or heal the tribe. WIYS had that kind of implication too.

CA: I talked to a trainee and she said that monks use a kind of Walking in the monastery, too. They have a special place in the monastery for that matter, where they Walk, sometimes for a long period of time.

Joseph: Walking meditation?

CA: Yes, Walking meditation, it has a long tradition, and also pilgrimage, where people get in touch with certain spirits or God, has a long Walking tradition, hasn't it?

Joseph: Absolutely! The Walking is very active and makes you participate, I mean the Walks that they do on a pilgrimage in India, where they do prostrations, thousands of them or hundred thousands of them, where you Walk one step by going down, laying down on the ground and coming up again, and that's just a single step on their long way. And you do this all the way to the Himalaya. Wow! Indeed it is a way to bring yourself to another way of knowing, another way of being. So there is a tradition of the Walking in many cultures.

CA: It looks like there is a long tradition, but we didn't call it "Walking." It had and has different names …

CA (next question): How has Walking-In-Your-Shoes changed your life? I assume it did.

Joseph: That's a very difficult question to ask, actually. I have seen thousands of Walks … It's a real challenge, I could start talking but it would take me 15 minutes to get through that answer. I guess the real question for me is: If I hadn't done Walking would my life be any different? I would say, if empathy is something that you can develop, to feel with others and other beings, I think the practice of Walking certainly has strengthened and help me grow in terms of my compassion for others. If that were the only thing that it did, that would be enough, for having worked with it for 20 years or so.

By Walking other people I found that I could trust my inner being to be a revealer, to reveal things for other people. It allowed me to experience energies that I hadn't ever touched before. Difficult things also, pain and joy, great joy. I'd say that in some ways it helped me be a lighter person. I think I was always considered somewhat "heavy," you know, or serious. I think Walking certainly helped me shake a lot of that out. I think it freed me as a person and as a performer, too. Performing and being an actor and a creative person was always my passion. I think the Walking helped push that out a little further, maybe a lot.

It enabled me to encounter so many different types of people, so many different walks of life. People I would have never met without the Walking. But I think I am better for having met them, and Walked them, and they Walked me. Having used the Walking and practice it … and practice it more, gives me an experience, something that is usually philosophical, do you know what I'm saying? I guess that's the same as experiencing a certain stillness in meditation. By Walking other people, I got to see that there is something about our humanity that is very common, very much shared. Our humanity is shared, there isn't anything inside me that isn't inside you.

John Cogswell would say, that one of the reasons why we believe Walking works, is because there is an essential "oneness" of all things, that we are essentially ONE. Humans are one, the trees and the rocks and the plants, we're all one. This is a fairly high religious concept, certainly with Buddhism, Christianity as well, that there is a oneness, that really is our essential nature. When we use the Walking, we're tapping into that very oneness. It is really no miracle, the fact that we can reveal each other and that we can be of service to each other, because at the heart of things we really ARE each other anyway. So, I've got a chance to experience that, rather than read it in a book.

CA: Great! Joseph, I would like to know which Walk has influenced you the most?

Joseph: A Walk that impacted me recently just happened the other night. A woman came to the group for the first time. And when a new person comes to the group, I often say: "To give you an impression about the Walking, I want to invite you to ask us to Walk someone that you know."

I don't always ask them to be Walked themselves directly, because that can be a little assaulting, for some people too much. But I say:

"… just to show you that we have faith in this process, because it does seem to work, tell us someone that you know, it could be a loved one, could be a friend, a problem figure, it could be someone who's alive or passed away, it doesn't matter."

And so she suggested someone, Diana, and one of our members of the group got up and said okay, I am now Diana, without knowing anything about her. He (the Walker) felt kind of exited, rejuvenated, refreshed, and he felt very light, floating. He just seemed to skate around the room. He said: "I'm flying and floating, I feel like I'm not quite on the ground. And I like it." He kept being struggling, saying: "… you want me to be something more angst-ridden, or have a problem, but I don't really feel it, right now. I don't really feel I have a problem." He finally tried going down on the ground and laying there for a while and saying: "Well, I guess if I made myself back in this place I would feel stuck and angry and I am sort of blaming you for putting me here. But I'm not here anymore. I have a choice." And he got up and started floating around again.

Well, the woman then told us after the Walk that this was her mother who had passed away about 12 years ago. I just thought that was remarkable. And I know that the Walker was really impressed by it, too. Certainly, you can read this anyway you want, but it was meaningful for her and she felt that a lot of his (the Walker's) qualities not only were the qualities of how she might imagine her now if she'd passed away and was free of some of her earthly problems. But there were also qualities that she felt that he exhibited that were her in life, too, which was her sense of humor, a very willingness to not get too caught up in things. So, there were a lot of benefits for her to see her mother Walked. And he, the Walker, was very expanded, I think, in his own way. So I went away from that session just thinking that was really remarkable. It would have never happened if someone hadn't decided to Walk … I just wanted to tell you that one …

CA: *Can you give us another example?*

Joseph: You know I have several examples, many actually, written down (thinks …). Yes, I'll talk about when I Walked my mother.

CA: Is your mother still with us?

Joseph: ... and my mother is not with us, and she was not at that time as well. The thing I really got from that was, I had experienced my mother as a child and as a young man in a certain way. And then she passed away. In many ways I never really felt like I knew her. We didn't really have time as adults to get to know each other. I knew her the way a child knows, certain moods and attitudes and things about her parents ... And I had issues as well because of things that happened.

So, in a way I might have had resistance to trying to Walk her. And I get this a lot from people, It's like, "I don't really want to Walk the person that I have a problem with, because it's more important for me to have that problem and define myself against that person." That's of course is a trap that we all fall into. But it's scary, I think. In a way WIYS requires you to open yourself in a way that you might not be comfortable doing, because you think you're going to give up something. Which you do!

So, when I Walked my mother, I was very surprised that I felt instantly not like her as an adult! I felt that I was a little girl! I felt very small, quite vulnerable, and it was so clear that I wanted my dad to love me, like me. Her issues, which preceded me, were so difficult and terrible with her own parents. And what I got was an experience of that! It really gave me a lot more compassion for her. I feel it even now when I talk about it! All my complaints that I may have had about my parents and my mother were valid, but what I got was a compassion about who she was. That was hidden from me. I never knew that!

You could argue I might have had some information about her, but I didn't experience her that way. When I decided I would *be* her, I said: "I am now Nancy." it flooded me with a whole other awareness of what it must have been like *to be her*.

Years later, working on a play, in the middle of a performance, I remember that. It was very powerful in terms of what I was accessing, emotionally and in terms of my point of view, on stage, and it was because of my understanding of that Walk. I'll always have a sense of that because of the Walking.

115

CA: I can see that it touches you now a little bit.

Joseph: It does. It still does.

CA: So that was profound.

Joseph: That was very profound.

CA: Could you maybe tell us another moving example?

Joseph: You're welcome. The following story, for example, has greatly influenced my creativity: We were working with a writer who was working on a character. That's part of how I applied the Walking, to help him. So I said the character's name was "Martin." And that was all I said. And our job was just to Walk and see what happens. So now we're really pushing the boundaries of Walking, when we say that all you have to do is tell us the name and something in this room will happen, IF we drop our agendas, IF we let go of our egos and just do it, then something will be revealed.

Four or five people Walked, one after another, this character. I think the first one was, that he had some sort of mission. He was on that mission and he was going to perform that mission. Nothing was going to stop him from that.

Then another person got up and Walked, and she felt that she had to lead people somewhere, to a certain destination. There was responsibility for that leadership and she was also responsible for those people. The Walker was worried if he would do a good job or not. But he felt that it was his responsibility.

Yet another felt that, whatever happened, he felt like he had not long to live and that everything would happen in God's hand and that it was okay.

CA: And did you all Walk the same character?

Joseph: All Walking the same character! And each time something else arrived, each time something else came out of the Walk. Again, another person Walked and he felt that he was also something like a public image. He was a family person, and he was also kind of "lusty" at the same time, he had a certain sexual drive. Anyway, finally we all sat down and the guy said it was "Martin Luther King Jr. …"

What have we seen? The role was that he would lead people somewhere, he was convinced that he had a mission to fulfill, that "they" weren't important but the mission was really important. He had a family, he had a love life. And all these things came out of just really nothing, you know, no one was trying to guess. We were just doing the Walking and still it brought out the themes, and the writer was able to take notes. It really supported him on his work on the piece.

I thought that was wonderful. It was just great! It was an opportunity for us to just trust our own being and our own commitment to the moment. And for him it was a chance to let go and let other people work with his material. I think that's very healthy. And it all comes back together. I like this story.

CA: What is your most important experience with this method?

Joseph: (thinks for a long time) I cannot answer the question. I have the impression that there is a growing realization process. I have been doing this job for many years now. I had the opportunity to do many Walks. It seems like having an accumulating effect in terms of my abilities as a person and a performer, as well as just growing. I know I am better for having used the work and followed it.

We were talking earlier: If a problem comes up, Walk it! (… laughs …). I think it's really a good tool. Part of the good lesson of the Walking is that it's all happening here and now, right now. You decide that you want to do it and you Walk and something will appear to you. You know, it's a way to cut right through and get to the point. Instead of years of therapy and sitting around talking about things,—just get up and Walk it,—and you might have a chance of integrating this missing piece. That in itself is a gift, I think. I am not going to say that I can bring it down to one great experience that was life-changing. It's been more like an adventure, a journey.

CA: That's a great answer! What was your funniest or your worst experience with the Walking? Was there something where you had to laugh, or something that really went wrong?

Joseph: Oh my goodness …

CA: Did that happen?

Joseph: Well, many things have happened during Walking.

CA: The great experiences you won't forget, I guess?

Joseph: No, you do not forget the valuable lessons learned usually. There were plenty of difficult situations during Walking ... One of my favorite stories: I found the situation hilarious and at the same time it was another great Walk that has pushed me forward in my thinking and in my understanding of the process. One of the tricks of Walking is to undermine one's own self-judgment. And that many people find difficult to do, for most of us. To stop the inner voice that persuades one: "Oh, that's only me, who makes up stuff and it's not really authentic, it is not good, it is boring. "You know, all this stuff with which we undermine ourselves. Don't undermine yourself, instead: You have to find a way as a Walker to put that aside! And a good example is this funny situation:

A woman was asked by a man to Walk his uncle, his uncle Earl. She got up and said, "I am now Uncle Earl" and immediately began to shoot across the room. She was trying to get something and trying to feel something. She tried to exert herself to be uncle Earl. Finally, she was completely frustrated and said: Oh, I cannot do it! I cannot do it! I cannot do it! I'm a fake, I'm a fraud, it's all just invented! I don't know how to do this. I cannot be Uncle Earl. It's just me trying to make something happen! I can't do it!

And the man jumped up and shouted: That's him! That's it! That's uncle Earl! That's the way he was! He was a businessman, a Japanese businessman, his whole life, who struggled all his life to conform to the image that he had about himself and the image his family had of him. He never made it, and always felt like a failure.

I just said, mark this down! Because even though this woman was doubting her own ability to Walk, she still found out what happened in the Walk. She was frustrated and thought she could not do it, but still, she embodies all the qualities of Uncle Earl. So let me put it this way: Basically, there is Walking with more benefit or with less benefit. I say this because I believe that Walking always has a benefit. But you get less benefit from the Walking if you spend time in the Walk criticizing yourself and believing that it's you, not the person that you are Walking. There is a little trick of the mind. But you can make up your mind to turn the whole thing and say, when I perceive feelings of self-doubt, or do not know what I'm doing, then I'm just going to assume that that's part of the character of the person I'm Walking and include that as part of my Walk.

By embracing it, you're going to give the most benefit to the person you're Walking. If you play games with yourself and decide arrogantly want is you and want isn't you, you are not helping the person you are Walking. You are holding something back. So give it up! Let it go and embrace everything, even if it feels so familiar that it couldn't be the Walk. You're not the person who decides.

I love this Walk. It is very instructive.

Interview part 2, on March 22ⁿᵈ 2009 in Joseph's apartment in Santa Monica, California

CA: What was the worst experience you've ever had?

Joseph: The worst experience? Let's see. When I think of a few Walks, which were very enlightening and really helped me trust in the process, I can think of quite a few extraordinary experiences. For example, one time a guy asked us to Walk his father. A woman stood up and Walked his father without knowing anything about him. Immediately she felt a strong weakness in her legs, as if they were going to give out, at any moment. The woman wanted to explore that feeling a little closer and find out why her legs were so weak. She therefore turned to a chair. Soon she began to push the chair and said. "I want to keep Walking, but I'm going to take the chair to help me steady myself," she also said some other things, and then the Walk was over. When she sat down again, the man explained, "My father is sick and cannot use his legs, he uses a walker." That was an eye-opener, in which we asked ourselves how can that be? What is happening? She could have Waked anything and she got that!, but it was precisely this physical weakness that had shown itself.

Another time, a man asked us to Walk his son Pablo. He had not seen his son for several years. Pablo lived with his mother somewhere in New Mexico. As we Walked Pablo, several people felt that he had a real difficult spirit, and that he was in great turmoil. Someone found a bottle of beer, he played with it and took a sip. The man finally said, " You know that my son is an alcoholic? He drinks and constantly gets in trouble." Then he went home after the Walk and found a message on his answering machine from his son. His son had not called in five years, and now the day had come! His son called that day! Maybe you can understand that we all got goose bumps?

These are the kind of Walks that make you really question: Wow! What are we dealing with here? How can it be possible that you could just state someone's name in a given moment and move, and things appear, things get revealed. These exciting Walks inspired me and make me want to experiment further.

Then there also were very strange and weird Walks that were some-how "off," where the craziest things happened. Once a guy was Walking a woman whose husband had just died. He as the woman was not afraid to get right into the role, into her sexual organs, into her sexuality. He said: " I feel that all this energy wants to come out, come out of my vagina! "- I remember that we were all a bit tense. It's like, poor woman, we don't even know her, and what is he doing, it's terrible? And the man as the woman said -" I feel all this energy coming out of my pussy! I need to get involved in this energy, I have to share it with people. Here is my strength, my energy."

When he finally sat down, we turned to the woman. She was pretty taken aback by it. I feared that this Walk had been so disgusting for her, that she would leave any moment. She really was in deep grief. I suspect that she was not sexually active for some time and that a lot of energy had been stored. It's hard to believe, but she was open to it and took it in.

Later, she came back and said: " This Walk was very meaningful to me, this particular Walk. I don't know if I was completely ready for it when it happened. But it had a lot to do with my ability to move forward and embrace a lot of who I am, it gets really cut off at times." She went on and had a full career as a therapist, helped a lot of people and be very dynamic in her own way.

There was something about the Walker's willingness to go ahead with what was happening with him and trust, even if he didn't understand it, that it might have some relevance. It was a scary moment, but it turned out to be really meaningful for that woman.

One could say that the other side of the quality of Walking is "risk." Because we are really going to risk everything. You risk making a fool of yourself. You risk being really ridiculous in the way we normally think of ourselves. You're assuming you could tap into somebody else. You risk a lot in terms of your ego, and maybe even hurting somebody.

These experiences have taught me a lot about the element of risk of Walking and yet—trust. Trust is really the key.

I remember one time, a participant came to a Walking group and her buttons were really pushed. We Walked each other, we Walked ancestors, we Walked different characters. And it really bothered her after a while. Somehow it violated what we were doing, because it was against her religion. The woman was Catholic. To her it seemed as if we were playing around with something obscure, dark. She said: " It's like voodoo, I cannot go along with this. I'm going to leave." Then she got up and walked out. That was really the only time that such a thing happened.

CA: And did she come back?

Joseph: She never came back. But that's okay, I accept that. In my memory we touched some topics that were very close to her heart: who she was, where she came from, who she wanted to be, etc. And all this was in conflict. Like I said, it was the only time anyone has walked right out.

The importance of that, if there is any: Walking challenges some of our most fundamental beliefs about reality and about what we think is possible. We grow up believing that everything is separate.

This is a strong core belief, a big assumption. It influences how we live our lives, how we perceive reality and ourselves. We experience ourselves as two different entities, which are separate: My body—your body. Walking seems to be a bridge to a completely different way of thinking, a different way of being in the world. We are not as separate, really. On the one hand it is liberating, but at the same time, it's challenging.

I have this body, I have my experiences, I live my own life. That makes me unique. And the same goes for you. You have your memories, I have mine and they are not the same. And yet there is something that the Walking brings up, like an innate ability, something that is characteristic in our existence, it is an ability to feel commonality and to "see" and to be of service. We can mirror each other and help each other in this way.

I think it would be wrong to say we are all the same. We are not the same. But there is a level of unity that we do share. At this level we are one and everything is possible.

CA: And we need a technique that brings it out, such as the Native American do?

Joseph: That's right. All these techniques we can use to get in touch with this innate quality or gift, whatever you want to call it. I believe that modern spiritual exercises such as meditation can help it. Sometimes it happens quickly, sometimes it takes a long time. Beliefs about reality, about ourselves, are deeply rooted in us. They are practically part of ourselves. "Practice" is the way to learn that there is a different way of looking at things.

I say this, because what we found with the Walking is—a lot of resistance. Resistance is a very important subject when it comes to Walking: People can take part in a weekend workshop. They see and do amazing things. They can Walk as other people or they can be Walked. They feel accepted and embraced and really experience significant breakthroughs. But don't be surprised if they do not come back. Maybe not for a long time, perhaps they never come back. Even though they can have that enlightening experience, it doesn't mean they can make it part of their lives. Because it does challenge how we live. It must!

If we were to do Walking or Constellation work all the time or every day, it's going to change you. Your point of view changes, your heart, your compassion may change, the way you treat other people. It has to! Once you start to see, everyone is kind of united on some level, you can't treat people the same way as you might have before—or yourself! But those habits are hard to break. I've seen both. I have seen people who have taken up the Walking and it changed their lives, went on with it and it was great. I have seen others who thought it was amazing and were enthusiastic about the Walking and have never done it again.

In any case, it shows how powerful the practice of Walking really is. At the same time, it's not as easy as to learn how to brush your teeth. You have to find a way to practice regularly and that's not easy to do. In my opinion it is best done in a group. Of course you can do it alone or with a friend. But usually, you still need someone else to hold the space and keep the energy.

All practices need time to take root. Psychotherapy is only about 100 years old and now widely accepted, even if not everyone does it. Maybe there will be some Walking centers one day, where people can come along and say: "I'm now gonna do some Walking today! (laughs loudly ...), and it will be completely normal. But we're not there yet.

In the Walking centers you will find classes like Family Constellation and Walking groups, and you go to workshops ... Those who are interested can go there, get trained or attend a workshop. It just needs someone to implement this into practice.

CA: I think this will probably happen.

Joseph: Yes, I think it will happen, and I think it can! In any case, and it should happen.

CA: This is why it is important for me to be a part of letting other people participate in Europe also. Not because it's for me, not for me, but to have other people access this method and get interested.

Joseph: Perhaps you remember when Peter Levin began with his trauma therapy 10-15 years ago, he was the only one who offered the "Somatic Experiencing." There was one book—and that's it. Now the method is widespread. In many places you can learn about the method.

It's now a recognized movement. What's the next question? Are you still recording?

CA: Have I asked you: What do critics say about the Walking?

Joseph: That's very important. I've heard different opinions. One must not forget that Walking is an entirely subjective matter. The people who are Walking have an experience that they feel valid. They have an experience where their experience is shifted, simply by making the statement of intention and moving in their body. They have the experience that something happens to them that is new and different. This has validity for them.

Also the person who is watching, who is being Walked, has an experience that is valid to them, that is meaningful. Through empathy and compassion and the feeling of oneness, they feel embraced, they feel very accepted, they feel they have been kind of celebrated in some way that they never had felt before.

What hasn't happened yet with Walking-In-Your-Shoes is, there has never been a study. There is no quantifiable evidence yet that's been shown, that people agree, this has a benefit. I have personally observed changes in the lives of the participants, but this is a pretty vague statement. There are no quantifiable surveys that show that. How can one even quantify the Walking, how can you measure it? A scientific study would have to be sought. But even that would be based on the feeling of the people. I do not believe that you can measure it somehow.

CA: I think it would be feasible. This could be an experimental group of about 100 people. This group would be interviewed maybe two or three weeks before the Walk, then directly before the Walk, while Walking, immediately after the Walk, and again six weeks later. And then evaluate and describe what this test group has said.

Joseph: This is what needs to happen! Because it is a study and we could have some evidence to point in some direction. But because I cannot show that to anybody right now, all you can do is come in, and experience it, and see what it is for you or listen to what someone might say about it.

One criticism certainly is that anything the person does in a Walk has aspects of humanity that are common to anybody. Therefore, the person who is observing can say: Yes, sure, that is me, or that is my grandfather or that is … whatever, and find things to agree with.

CA: Like a horoscope does?

Joseph: Yes, like in a horoscope.

CA: What I mean is, you can read the horoscope of somebody else and still say, yes, that's me.

Joseph: Right. You could read anything into the Walk that has common features or properties of humanity. Our tendency is, that we're going to agree. As we keep looking for common ground, of course, there is a tendency to find similarities and agreement, that one could express as, "everything goes."

But I would take issue with that. For I have seen things in Walks that are entirely specific to the person that has been Walked. Entirely specific to that person's family. The Walker could never know! All they have is a name! There are no visual cues, nothing to go on. So I want to stop and ask, well, why did the person Walk that quality? Thousands of other properties could have been Walked. But that one, the one you get, is entirely specific to that person who is Walked. I have a hard time believing that this is just coincidence. This is based on my long experience in having seen hundreds of Walks. If I could, I would say that 90% of all Walks are pretty accurate and specific.

Of course, it also happens that people do not immediately see anything, however, I will say that some of those people have come back later and said, you know, what we Walked really did have relevance later on. Like the woman of whom I told you, the Walk that was very sexual. She didn't know how to relate to that, but later on, she realized that the Walk was crucial and had incredible relevance for her in how to know where she was going.

So, I always say, "If you don't see anything now—think about it. Come back later and tell me if it had any meaning. Upon greater reflection the person will find what is true about the Walk.

Again, the critics will say, that it's just anything, there is no such ability that people have. Even if that were true, and we'd have neither the ability to mirror each other, nor tap into some collective knowledge, I would still say: It doesn't matter. Which maybe isn't the right thing to say.

But the fact remains that there still is a group of people that has come together, and somehow they're healing each other. In the end it does not matter whether we are great psychic beings. We have the firm intention to be each other and something good is coming out of it. Of course, I would rather prove to you that there is a larger and deeper force at work here, that we are all part of a field, and therefore have access to each others being. I discount the people trying to discredit it, because in the end I've seen so many good things happen, that it wouldn't really matter.

I don't consider Walking to be a religion, but if we took a religion: Take for example the Christian faith. If I postulated, "I can prove to you that there is no personal God, that is a personage, and that your prayers are not answered by any supreme being," can you prove me otherwise? But this doesn't reduce the incredible benefits that people get from saying prayers and praying for each other and being kind to each other, because they believe that there is an afterlife (laughs). It's quite funny, because in the end you come back to the same issues about any kind of spiritual practice, saying: "Even though I cannot prove it right now, I believe there is something good about it."

I think that a study of Walking would bear out the benefit. If it couldn't prove anything else, it would show a benefit. Perhaps this is the most important.

CA: Do you really need to be so modest about the Walking?

Joseph: I don't need to do that, but I thought a lot about it. I want to be honest about it. I know what I see. It's a good question. I guess, I am trying to deal with people's cynicism and say: "If I can't prove it to you, at least see the results in the people." And maybe that's the only good point.

CA: So are you saying: If you can't prove that god exists, at least those guys could be a good Country Club?

Joseph (laughs loudly): Richard Dolphin says, even if someone does

126

not believe in God, he can still be overwhelmed by the beauty and the incredible diversity of nature and its breathtaking complexity. This experience is sacred and has a kind of sacred quality in itself. If you're really getting into it, you encounter the holy.

CA: Have you ever had a Walking representative who had trouble doing the Walk? Can you give another example?

Joseph: That's important. Obviously there is a range of problems that can come up when someone is trying to do a Walk. One difficulty we have just discussed: When you're getting in your own way. This happens when your thoughts about what you're doing is more important than what you're doing. And that you are being self-critical and you are sort of keeping yourself separate from the Walk. This obstacle must be overcome in saying: "Even as I doubt, I am willing to include that doubt as part of this Walk." The instruction is always: Be with what is! Don't make up anything. Be with what is! Your feelings, your thoughts and how you want to move. Pay attention to what is happening in the moment. That is something you can learn to train yourself to get over it. Just by accepting what is. Accepting your thoughts and what's happening.

Another difficulty may arise in this context, in people with a weak sense of their self. In other words, their sense of self is fragile and somehow wounded. I mean everybody is wounded in some way, but these people do not want to Walk as someone else. It is a form of self-ishness. They fear being overwhelmed or taken over by someone else. They don't want to spend time serving someone else. They want it for them; they want benefit for themselves. And this is where that person may be in their development.

I, of course, encourage you stepping out of even that! Stepping out of that limitation and Walk as someone else and see what happens. But some people are frustrated with that, they really want to be served themselves. If that happens, there are other ways to apply the Walking. That is why I advocate this person can Walk as an archetype, a hero, a god or goddess, something of that nature to help them lift themselves or embrace more of themselves. Obviously, you can have them Walk as their higher self. That sometimes is appealing to people who get stuck in the feeling: they don't get enough. And certainly you can have other people Walk them, which makes them feel embraced.

I think you need a strong sense of yourself in order to step away from it! But maybe that's a semantic problem. Someone who does not want to Walk someone else, has a very strong sense of his own self. The ego may be perhaps wounded, but it is very strong. They can still benefit from Walking as another. But this can be a difficulty. You must find ways to deal with it.

Or when someone is holding on so much to themselves that they just can't let go to become the person they're Walking, it's getting difficult. They just cannot stand departing from themselves in any way.

CA: Or, they are not able to?

Joseph: No, they are not.

CA: In one case there was somebody who was trying, with all his might, to hold the image that he had of himself, as a kind of survival strategy. He couldn't do a Walk at all.

Joseph: As a kind of protection?

CA: Yes, you could say that. But this man never noticed that about himself.

Joseph: I think that you can work with them anyway. Sometimes you get people who think: it's all them, it's all them; there is a woman in my workshop right now, who is just like that. It's always them, this isn't someone else! So the way I work with her is saying: "Just get in touch with what is happening. Stop saying it isn't and it is! What happens now? Where are you now?" If someone stays with the work over a longer period of time, they'll loose that discrimination. Instead of just saying: "that's me, that's just me ...", ask yourself: "OK, well, what is happening? Aha, so you feel so tense. Aha, so you feel rigid. Aha, so you feel you can't move, etc. Let them go through that! It may not yet be the Walking that we're looking for, but this exercise will strengthen their body awareness. You can encourage people to appreciate their value even more. They'll experience that, what they have, is already valuable. After some time, they will not judge so much to say but,

"Well, I'm now Walking as that person and let me Walk with what is. I'll stay with that, and that's valuable."

This goes back to our conversation about Walking with less benefit or with more benefit. Because the more we keep stuck in our own impressions of what we think we are and what we think the Walk might be, the less benefit is has. It's not helpful. Once you let go and you say: "I feel tense. I feel self-critical. I feel judged all the time ... whatever it is ... that's what I'm Walking." That will have more value to the person you're Walking.

Another issue that is a problem for people is: extrapolation. Extrapolation means: drawing lots of conclusions from a little bit of information. I'll give an example: Someone says, "I feel kind of bent over. A little bit like I am crippled or something." Then the Walker begins to imagine these qualities: he suggests that he uses a cane, he says "I feel like a witch, like a green witch ..." and so on. And they're Walking someone that's right there in front of them. Then I stop and say "I appreciate that you are feeling these things, but you don't have to turn it into a performance. Try to figure out what it means, on an emotional level, that you cannot move or that you just feel crippled. Don't turn it into a character for me right now." That can push someone away. I would say to the Walker: "If you want to Walk for the benefit of another person, you need to do so with reverence. This does not mean that you should hide what's going on inside you. No, show it openly, reveal it. But be aware that you are there for the benefit of someone else.

Extrapolation is especially tempting for actors. As performers they are trying to be interesting and colorful. So that's a type of extrapolation of what's happening, you try to build on it and improvise further. In a role, a character, an archetype or something imaginary that's fine. But if you are Walking the grandmother of a participant or a person who is present, then I advise to refrain from such images. Report only what is happening, rather than invent stories like: "I live in a castle, and there runs a moat. There dwells a dragon and now I am running over the fields ..." I stop and say: "Well, now you are here in this room. You

are feeling swept away by your thoughts? See if you can identify that."
So I bring people back to the moment.

CA: What needs to be said or done before working with first-timers, participants who attend for the first time?

Joseph: When I work with people for the first time, it is important to understand that we want to make a statement of intention, and everything that comes after that is to be considered part of the Walk: The characteristics, the qualities, feelings or thoughts of the person you're Walking. I say for example: "Even if you think it's just you, and you have those thoughts. Let the doubts that may come up be part of Walk. Don't stand outside of it. Try to let go of calling on any preconception about what you are Walking. Just be in this moment. Notice how your body will move in that moment, and what is now. Your attention should be focused on the present moment, go to your intention and what comes up for you. Try to follow the impulses as best you can. Take your time. When the impulses come up, how do you want to move, explore them in more detail and share your perception, the best you can. If you encounter a limitation and you get stuck, ask yourself what's missing. Usually there is some place in your body, in your thoughts, or in your energy, that has not yet been expressed and explored. This could be the opposite of what you're doing, or it could be a drag or a resistance. This area could manifest as fear or anxiety. Feel closer, go into that and ask "What do I say to this missing piece? What is it saying to me?" I want to invite them to go into that, because often that is important information. And then finish whenever it seems right. So that's what I do, I give a brief overview of what I expect or where they need to put their intention.

CA: I have had several people who felt that we are entering a much too personal level in a Walk, and because we are able to tap into things and go deep, we could be able to see things that the person who was Walked maybe never would have revealed or shared with us. Do you see a danger in Walking-In-Your-Shoes?

Joseph: Where are the dangers in this process? I think a lot of what we have just discussed is applicable to that. You cannot assume that you are going to tap into the innermost anything of this person! This is not for you to assume! We are not calling you a psychic, we are not calling you a mind reader. You are simply getting up to do a service by Walking and embracing this new moment however it manifests, and see if you can follow it.

I try to keep people away from making up stories about what they think, what their brain is carrying on, based on a few impulses. I call this extrapolation: making things up, drawing conclusions from very little information. What you could stay with is, that your hands feel like ringing or waving themselves and you may feel nervous and the hands may want to seek help. Stay with the emotional, mental and energetic position of where you're at.

You may have images come up, some people are very visual in their brain. You can say, okay you have images, maybe you can share some of these images. But it's not for you to assume that you are now the mouthpiece or the spokesman of that person. You won't know that until later, after the person has given some feedback. The feedback is an essential part of the process, absolutely important. You Walk as someone, you sit down and you ask: "What I just did, did that have any meaning for you?" Because it may not have. You should have to hear that, too. The person will then feed back to you the things that did have meaning and hopefully you will gain more trust in the process.

Your attitude has to be very open and not assuming that you have now come to know the innermost thoughts and feelings of the other person. Otherwise you can get into trouble there. You could make up stories. I'll tell you what it can do: It'll make that person feel that you have a personal opinion about them. And that's not safe. That can be a danger. But I think it's just a question of technique, the way to practice, the way to do it.

CA: In one of my workshops a participant wanted to have her co-worker Walked. In that Walk we saw that on the inside the co-worker was more in contact with the dead than with the living. For the women it was difficult to see that. She feared that this information gave her more knowledge about the co-worker than she had asked for. Do you see what I mean?

Joseph: Yes, I understand. The question here is what you do with the information? And how we evaluate the information? That could be a danger. We need to consider very carefully what information we want to take literally. Many things that come up in the Walking are often metaphoric and symbolic in nature. They should be taken on an emotional level, not necessarily on the level of facts. There is no possibility for you to check the information. You could of course address the co-worker directly and say: "By the way, could you tell me, if you are perhaps in contact with the spirit of the dead?" That's possible (laughs). But I think that's not valuable.

That is not the question to which the woman is seeking an answer. In my opinion, this is an issue of how to process information therapeutically. If you have difficulties with a co-worker, you want to see somebody Walk her, the intention is to open the compassion to that person, not your judgment, and if you are judging the person, that's still an issue and the Walking may not be able to solve that entirely. That, you would have to work on yourself, in your own time. Although the Walking usually is a doorway for more compassion and more empathy for other people.

It also raises the question of whether Walking is suitable for everyone? I would say yes. We have already talked about the fact that the habits of mind cannot change so quickly. Those are the things you have to work on over much longer periods of time, usually, … your habits of mind.

CA: What is your vision for the future of this work? How might this work look like in 5 or 10 years?

Joseph: On the one hand, I hope that we will receive research funding for further study and see what kind of results can come from that. I'd love to see some real data of one hundred people who are Walked or do Walking. What benefits it has, if any. What do they see? How does it effect them? How did it change their lives?

CA: Would you carry out such a study yourself?

Joseph: I do not know if I'm qualified enough as a researcher. In any case, it takes time and energy. If I had the money, I'd do it, surely. But I'd love to farm it out to someone who might even be very dispassionate about the Walking, someone who is familiar with psychological studies. This would certainly be very helpful in making it happen.

The second would be a kind of Walking center. Such a center could also provide other forms of individual and group work, such as Family Constellation, in addition to Walking. And people could come and take workshops in the Walking. People could train to facilitate and give seminars and workshops to the public, so that it becomes a little more rooted in the culture. I know maybe five or six people who use the Walking in their practice and in their work. To me it should be much wider than that. Having a Walking center of that kind would be great. I'd love to see that happen.

Push forward on a film documentary would be interesting. It would be a very interesting subject. I have a lot of video footage. Just take a little budget, put it together and make a decent film. These are the practical and obvious things.

On a wider level, I would like to see Walking in the schools. I worked with Inner-City-Youth teenagers, 15-17 years of age, who have grown up in really difficult situations. They had no problems with Walking, none! "You are going to Walk your buddy?" The teenagers just jump up and do it! They didn't think about it, had no problems with it, didn't play games with it … They took right to it, without over-thinking, they just got into their bodies, their emotions, it had meaning for the friends that they were Walking. It brought them a sense of togetherness and closeness. So who knows … they now teach yoga in some schools and even meditation, I've heard, because it helps the children to be quiet and concentrate. So there might be classes in Walking, which not only is physical, which is good for the kids, but it's also getting them to recognize that the whole body is the mind! They can know things in their fingers, their feet, their toes, that's where you can know, not just in your head. For this reason, I find it important that Walking becomes a natural part of our educational culture.

CA: How do you use "Walking-In-Your-Shoes" in your career as an actor?
Joseph: This is how it all began. It is because I was an actor and am an actor. I pretty much eat, sleep and breathe acting. When this idea came up, I thought spontaneously, that this could be a really great technique for actors. Acting in a way is empathy. It's all about your capacity to empathize with a character, to be in contact with your feelings. Certainly about stepping away from what you consider to be your self, your "street-self," and stepping into the shoes of another character.

Walking for me is like the essence of acting. Someone once said, Walking is likely to have been part of an ancient shamanic ritual that already was cultivated by cave-dwellers. They sat around the fire and told stories of their hunting. While they talked, they got up and became the beast, became the bison or the hunter ... Instant story-telling—and the willingness to do that.

Not to mention, as we spoke earlier, about the medicine man, who in a way goes into the person, in order to find what is missing. And then he shares it with the patient. He heals, by bringing it into consciousness.

For actors, Walking is essential. I think a lot of actors do it intuitively and automatically. In general, they do not practice it as a conscious technique. That's why I've been working so long with actors, directors and writers. Writers sit in front of their typewriter, or their computer, and are they trapped completely in her head. They do not get up from their seat and move around as their characters. By Walking, they could investigate other layers in their roles.

Regardless of which role I work on, I always make sure that I use the Walking. Sometimes I make several Walks for a roll, sometimes I use the theater group and let other people Walk the character that I'm going to play. Maybe I'll see something that inspires me and stimulates me. That becomes a kind of collective approach to your learning, about the character, about how to perform. I cannot say enough about how useful Walking-In-Your-Shoes is for an actor!

CA: Last question: Is there anything that you'd like to say to the reader in Europe?

Joseph: I would tell them: "You have picked up this book, because you have an interest in growing, in some way, and expanding your awareness or your consciousness in some way. Walking is a very simple yet profound practice! I urge you to seek it out and give it a try. You will find something meaningful for you, either by being Walked by another person, or by Walking someone else. I think that you may find some expansion, or other consciousness, or some confirmation of things you already suspect are true about reality. The reality is much more than what we see or think it is.

But these considerations remain abstract philosophy, as long as we do not find a way how to actually do them, to practice them, to find a practical way to live awareness. It is best to take part in a Walking workshop. Perhaps there is one in your city. And if not, please contact Christian Assel! He will give you some instruction. And see what this technique is all about.

Thank you so much, Joseph!

Interview with John Cogswell and Joseph Culp, the Founders of Walking-In-Your-Shoes

This is a transcribed interview from my audio recordings which was held in June 30th 2009 in John Cogswell's house in Santa Barbara, CA. The questions have been chosen by the author of this book.

Present are:

Joseph Culp (writer, director, actor and co-founder of Walking-In-Your-Shoes), since 1990 he offers workshops for actors and directors, 1992 establishment of the "Walking Theatre Group," more info on www.JosephCulp.com

John Cogswell, Ph.D. (Psychologist with many years of practice and co-founder of Walking-In-Your-Shoes), began his work in "Brattleboro Retreat" in Vermont, since 1959 Scientific Director of the "System Development Corporation in Santa Monica, CA, USA," worked for James F. Bugental, Ph.D. between 1965 and 1968, here he learns humanistic-existential psychotherapy and studied Jung. From 1982-2002 he studied Buddhism under the guidance of the venerable Tibetan Lama Rinpoche Gyatrul and makes his "Bodhisattva Vows," since 1993 publications on Walking-In-Your-Shoes, most recently he taught therapist colleagues in Walking-In-Your-Shoes in Los Angeles and Santa Barbara, CA, USA.

Christian Assel M.A. phil (Philosopher, trainer and facilitator in "Family Constellation work" and "Walking-In-Your-Shoes," founder of Walking-In-Your-Shoes in Europe).

Interview:

Joseph Culp (notes that John speaks very slowly and makes long pauses, John is in his 80's): I will say before we start that it might be useful and necessary for me to prompt or jump in during the interview.

Christian Assel: (to John) By the way, anything that you'll say, will make me be grateful! Thank you for letting me do this interview with you. I record the interview with this device, so I can write it down later. Okay. My first question is: How did you get in contact with Walking-In-Your-Shoes the first time, and when?

John Cogswell: Jo (Joseph Culp) was a part of this. What I have done a lot, is speaking from inside. And when I say this, there is another aspect. I came in contact with Tibetan Buddhists, and have spent about 30 years with them. I had wonderful trainers, and through them, I discovered a major focus, and an important aspect, which was the "oneness." This is a key issue. And many times I've been pushed in this direction and have felt humility, in being part of one, being part of all. I don't have an idea about me being somebody separate and competitive. The more I lived … (John lets me and Joseph, who are sitting on either side of him, take his hands … look out of the window, there are trees, the beauty, that you're here, and I'm here, (laughs) this is the oneness! And that means more than anything.

Joseph: And this orientation allows one to work therapeutically with people …

John: … with *everything*! …

Joseph: Walking-In-Your-Shoes is the result of this orientation. That was the primary understanding. And you, John, were doing the Walking in a sense, almost intuitively, already beginning to notice, that's the kind of work you will be doing. Just sitting with the client. And that you were able to identify things in your own body and speak from that, which was very revolutionary in my view, in terms of willingness to do that, saying: "I have a feeling here in my chest as I speak with you. And this is what it seems to be saying … " That is actually pretty presumptuous in comparison to the conventional therapeutic models.

CA: That interests me a bit more now. You, John, have spoken of "oneness," how did the "oneness" access the Walking method?

John: Well, it was actually the other way around. (laughs)

137

Joseph: The Walking has actually lead to a better understanding and experience of "oneness."

CA: So you've done the Walking first? (pause … all laugh loud.) Tough question, is it not?

Felice Cogswell, John's wife (briefly comes to us): Your teacher, the Tibetan Lama Gyatrul Rinpoche. Did he have something to do with it? With the "oneness?"

John: Yes, of course. He was my most important Tibetan teacher. A wonderful man, and he had a great sense of humor. Wherever he is now, I'm sure he still has it! (all laugh loudly)

CA: I like humor so much … it's so important.

John: Me too!

Joseph: I remember you, John, telling me about the understanding of "oneness," and that's part of the story that you have experienced, something important, in the course of your work as a psychologist in your spiritual development. That was an experience, years before, in an acting class, where you did an exercise in which participants would Walk through the room. That was like in the '60s. And John told me, during the

exercise, he observed changes inside, changes of his awareness, when he said he was going to Walk for someone else. Without trying to imitate anything, as actors do, he had a very physical and emotional awareness. Hence the idea to move and committing to another person and be in service for the other.

CA: So you were already given acting lessons?

John: I've always been acting! (everyone laughs loud, especially himself). I've always loved that, and to show off! (laughs again)

CA: How was the transition from those experiences to what is Walking-In-Your-Shoes today?

Joseph: Well, I'd like to answer the question, because I was not finished with my example. And maybe that will also answer the question. We had a session and we were working together. And one time you said, come on, let's try something here to maybe be able to spontaneously understand things without all the cognitive work and rather understand things with your body. Because I had gotten a role in a film, a role as a young priest. That was the moment where we actually put together the two things. I was an actor and he was a therapist. A marriage was born! (laughter) And he said, why don't you just get up right now and Walk this role? I already had some experience from acting roles, but I had learned that you need to understand things *before* you get up and go into the role. That is, philosophically speaking, exactly the problem. I had to know everything in advance, before everything begins, before I assume. But John said, no, just assume, just be this character! Someone wrote this character, probably it is based on something real, or something from the author's experience, so let's just assume it's real and you can just access that. And I said, well, ooookay, I'll try. After all we're doing therapy here ...!

I got up and began to have a real experience, and to this day it has been one of my most impressive experiences. It was great, energetic, I've seen things, I understood my relationship with the parents, and the Bible, and all the things about this character. You can now call it "Joseph's imagination went wild," or you can simply call it "permission." It was so powerful that I was ready to immediately play that character at any time. I almost did not have to read the script anymore. It was exciting and I was empowered by doing that. It was a significant part of the Walking, a kind of empowerment that the Walker gets about their abilities and the scope of who you are, as a being. That was the point at which it all began.

John: I feel soft in my heart area, I feel like crying. I feel loving. I like your smiles. Here are three people who are more conscious, more active, in a way ... When I heard there is a German coming here today, I thought, well, let 's see what's going to come from it, ... and more such bullshit (laughs) ... And as soon as I saw you ... I realized you're me too!! (all laughing beyond control, then we hug, all relax ...)

Joseph: When I look back on this event, I think of it as something groundbreaking. By the next month or so, you called me and said, why don't we do this more often. I'll call some friends and actors and we'll discover that a bit further. We had the first meeting in your home with

Jason, Robin and Greg, it was just the four of us and you. We met for several weeks, and that was really the conscious beginning of the work.
CA: So you were kind of testing it together?

Joseph: We started by Walking each other, each person would take a turn and we did multiple Walks for all. We started to see the benefit of being known—being known by someone. This was a new conscious thing, knowing each other in a direct way. We didn't say: "Now I'll tell you about my life" … no, that was not the case. It was about getting up and *being* you

John: And that's a *big* difference! (laughs) … big difference!

Joseph: It was very personal and intimate, it was right now. You were seeing things about you, which were known as your obstacles, and then again, other things which are your gifts and talents. That was amazing. Bringing out the essentials qualities of a person is a very empowering thing to the person watching.

CA: That's what I felt yesterday, when three Walks had been done for me in Joseph's workshop. Three different people Walked "me." It's very intimate. You are putting yourself out there on a very deep level and people get to know you really well. If they want to open up to it, they can. But today I have come to a point where I say, it's okay, I don't mind anymore.

John: Me, too!

CA: I have a life. And I might be the stupidest of all people, but if so, that's what I am. So why shouldn't everybody get to know me? Everyone has some kind of beauty, so why shouldn't people get to know me on this deepest level?

Joseph: Well, I think it's also a gift that you are allowing that to happen so it can inspire others. We can inspire others in saying: "What is it about you that you have to hide so much?"

John (to Joseph): I see so much of that it in you now. You're much more "out there," traveling, busy… .

Joseph: Yes, much more. I used to be more hidden. Maybe there was a good reason. But I no longer fear things the way I did, I think. And the practice of being "out there," makes me stronger.

John: I was glad to see you, and I was struck how clear you are. You are expressing yourself well … you are clearer, deeper …

Joseph: Yes, you know I'm happy today. I can now enjoy much more, and it's a relief to me (exhales deeply). I do not worry so much anymore. You know, many people are afraid and they want to hide, but it's actually a relief when you fully "come out." Sometimes in my workshop, I get a little dramatic when I say: "They're dead, and they came here to be alive again!" So be alive! They want you to be alive, don't hold back. They want to see your heart. And me too. In the theater it's the same. People looooove to see you when your heart is out. I do! If I go to the theater I want to hear something. I had my whole day and I'm tired, now show me something that is alive! And I would also say the same about the Walking. It has the same beneficial effect of being known ...

CA: John, when you were teaching Joseph in acting, had you already been a psychologist? Both at the same time?

John: Yes, I have worked as a therapist at the same time.

Joseph: Well, when you were doing the acting class, it was kind of a luck. You were doing therapy, and you were also in therapy, with James F. Bugental, right? There is an anecdote with you and Jim, that could be useful, in 1965 where you have had an experience of "oneness." This was a breakthrough, to which you have often related in writing. I think it has changed your perspective. You've written about it, right? (published by John Cogswell, under the title: "A Precaution"—author's note)

John: Oh, I have a stack of stuff and texts. I need to pull out some of that stuff again ... laughs.

Joseph: He immediately went to the research! (that makes John laugh) ... oh, I've got to get this ...

John: I have a stack of writing! Unfortunately I cannot read so well. But it's all about the Walking. There is some good stuff, I guess.

Joseph: Very good stuff ... One thing I've already spoken with Chris about, since he has really been proactive and writing a book and so forth, it's time for me to pull together what I've got and try to publish that too. Then America will have something and Germany will have something ... the book will be out ... (thinks) Maybe I need some of your material, John. (all laugh)

141

CA: I would love to read some of that too if you can make it possible? I would appreciate it.

John: I will. But I have a huuuuuge stack ... (laughs)

CA: Never mind. Whatever. Then we'll have something to pursue.

CA: I have an important question ...

Joseph (interrupts): How did you get to know Joseph Culp. That's the most important question ...! (all laugh)

CA: I'm sorry, I have to skip this question. (everyone laughs) But seriously, we have already talked about this question in the first interview. John, could you give us one or more Walking examples that you've seen as being especially beneficial or significant or meaningful?

John (thinks for a long time): Hmmm, now I have to explain my f+#*ing self (laughs out loudly), that's a pain in the ass! (laughs).

Joseph: (notes that John stumbles and jumps in ...) Well let's take one example. Maybe one that perhaps moved you, maybe one that stands out to you. I have told Chris about the Walk where I Walked my mother, which I did with you, John. A very, very significant Walk for me. Even when I speak of it now, I still feel emotionally moved by it. For the first time I could understand, and set aside, my resentment and release my anger towards her. I could be her, as a little girl, and have a father who was very, very harsh and difficult. And that was such a big part of her life. This opened my compassion for her, because she never got out of that! At least during my lifetime, this problem has never been released. The criticism of her father, the yearning for his love. It moved me to be more compassionate for her. John, do you remember the one client who sang, and always spoke so softly, and when she was Walking Barbara Streisand, she sang with this really powerful voice ...?

John: Yes, that's right (laughs).

Joseph: And this completely shocked you and her ... You should really pull out some of your notes ...

CA: How would you, John, explain the core of "Walking-In-Your-Shoes"?

John: The word "love" is really the core, the essence, and oneness (as he says that, the wind chimes in his garden started to make soft

142

sounds ...) You cannot be ONE, and not be loved (he puts his hands on the table, so that we can touch them. Joseph and I take his hands).

CA: That says a lot.

Joseph: Definitely.

John: It comes down to being the whole. Being one with conception, creation, birds (points to the birds behind the garden door), sky ... And there is also the awareness of the heart, and age. (laughs) O my god, what am I telling here? Now, I am smiling, and I feel a lot of freedom, even when I'm talking about death, too. It's a part of us. Sometimes I can't wait to finally get there ... (laughs loudly)

CA: Really?

John: Yes. I don't need to put any pressure on myself. Who knows where to go or what to do. On the other hand I am not going to escape. I am not looking for death to get away. I rather wonder what comes in the next chapter (laughs).

CA: We do not know, right? I sometimes wonder if there really is a next chapter? How do you see that, John? Do you believe in a next chapter?

John: I do, I do. Though I do not know. But I believe.

CA: I personally cannot remember a previous chapter of myself, so I don't know if there is a next one. I ask myself, if there was a next chapter, why can I not remember the previous one?

John: Well, I have the feeling that there already has been a previous chapter.

CA: What is that like and how does that feel?

John: I used to have a different family.

Joseph: So you are saying that you had a previous life. A lot of people have. Although there is no way to prove that. Buddhists believe that this orientation is beneficial for you to believe in. They say that everything you do has an effect on everything ...

CA: To be honest with you about that, when people refer to past lives, I always think they really refer to actual people from their own family. They think they have had past lives, but in reality they are in contact with real people from the past, perhaps a distant past. How do you see that?

John: "Oneness" pops up again. I've always been here.

Joseph: If you discover oneness, that is the experience. And that experience is not a mental hallucination. To say: "I have always been here, *this* has always been here, we have always been here, in various ways, perhaps as animals, … birds, the whole thing."

John: I wonder if that's more common in Germany?

CA: *Do you mean my perspective of past lives? That's hard to say. I can't say. Probably.*

John: I have not had so many clients from Germany. There are not as many over here. (laughs) But when I worked with Germans, I have found an iron strength, but locked. But I don't want to push anything onto you.

CA: *I know what you mean, I see it in myself and in my fellow countrymen. And my answer is that most of this is because of some of our past …*

Joseph: Okay, let's move on with the questions. (Joseph looks at the paper and reads the next question:) "What do the critics say?" And you, John, you had already taken notes in advance. What did you write down as an answer to that question? Let me see your paper *"The critics don't understand it!"* (all laugh beyond control)

CA: *Yes, I understand what you mean. No comment. But here is a question that is not on my list. A student of mine had asked: "What you are doing is pretty personal. So if I Walk my neighbor, then maybe I'll find out his secrets, those ones, he would never share with me. I would know things about him that he doesn't want me to know. Are you not going not too far here?"*

John: They are really tied up … (laughs)

Joseph: That sounds pretty head-tripping! The Walking is not at all about that. I would say to them: You are getting too much in your head, about … what if … and secrets … and stuff. Walking is to bring out intimate truths, of course, but also universal truths. You will not find out that your neighbor has stolen money from the bank or something. Well, I've never seen it.

CA: *We had a case once, where the co-worker of my participant, whom we Walked in my workshop, was in inner contact with all these dead people.*

That was strong and meaningful to my participant, knowing that about her co-worker. Now other participants asked, knowing this fact about the person, isn't that very personal and should it be revealed? Is that for us to know? We could take advantage of that.

Joseph: Was the co-worker present?

CA: No.

Joseph: And whoever Walked the co-worker said she was in contact with many dead people?

CA: Yes.

Joseph: My answer would be: "You don't know that!" You've discovered something that's important. But you to assume that it was a fact, may be an error in your thinking.

CA: Do you mean we don't know the truth?

Joseph: What I'm saying is, you are not looking at the whole, not deep enough. Some things in a Walk show themselves purely metaphoric. To assume that this is a fact, would be a literal interpretation. We can't assume that.

CA: Well, they would say that you do see facts, don't you?

Joseph: I think that's true. Nevertheless, you have to absorb the information to make it useful and beneficial for you personally. Otherwise, someone could come up to that person and say, "Hey, I Walked you the other day, and I saw that you're connected to dead people." We cannot do that!

CA: Is that a danger? Some could go as far as to believe that the CIA could use the Walking to spy on people. I could Walk in the role of a different government, trying to figure out what they are up to. You know, that's sometimes what people ask me.

Joseph: I know people have often said to me, well, Walking-In-Your-Shoes is like psychic. You're a psychic. The police employ psychics, etc. Maybe it's my way out of it, but I think no, it's not. There is no special skill. It is something that everyone has and can do. The point is not to collect information on a psychic level to assist people. It's about our own growth as a person. Does that make sense what I'm saying?

CA: Are you downplaying it now? What happens in a Walk is not ordinary, right?

Joseph: No, I think it is ordinary! I am not downplaying it. It's a gift, it belongs to everyone, because it's their very nature of oneness and being alive. But it needs to be developed. I do not see it the same way as guessing the cards on the table. The latter is psychic work. Which some people are very good at. You look at the cards, and there are three dots on a card in another room. I think that's also a skill that can be developed. But in Walking-In-Your-Shoes—maybe intention is a big part of this issue. But John says: intention is equal to love! So why are you doing this, why are you Walking? What are you up to?

CA: That's the point to where we had gotten, too, saying that you can only do this to help people. And that one must be clear about one's intention. You cannot do this without love.

Joseph: I think that's incredibly significant, the intention. I talked to Lauren, my wife, about this, about the atmosphere in the workshop, and that all participants need to feel safe. That should not be underestimated. The person leading the workshop needs to be skilled in "holding" the people, so that it's a safe place to be. All participants are mutually supportive, and we have to encourage that, and enhance that, in a workshop setting. Because people are dealing with enormous wounds, some don't know what to do with all this information yet ... But I mean, this is something I don't think about a lot. But it's very important.

CA: Talking of safety. Many workshop participants ask me about that, and I say: What happens in this room, stays in this room. This makes everyone feel safe.

Joseph: I think you're right. You create a "sacred" space. This is energy work here that's for your benefit, and hopefully for the benefit of others. You don't want to run around gossiping about this. I wouldn't mind saying that with a lot of seriousness. Gossip does hurt people.

CA: I usually take that for granted. How do you do that? Do you mention these things in your workshops, like privacy?

Joseph: Not always. People know it's a therapy session. But what you say, I find very important. People do have these conflicts.

CA: John, do you think that Walking can be dangerous?

John: I don't! That's not in my conscious repertoire.

Joseph: Walking another person is not dangerous.

CA: Have you ever experienced that a Walker had trouble getting out of the Walking role? (pause) I had it sometimes.

John: Really?

CA: Yes. Someone got into the role so much that he had difficulty leaving the role. Have you ever experienced this?

John: I don't remember such a thing.

CA: So this was obviously not a problem for you?

Joseph: I've had people be concerned about it. Perhaps this is what I hear you say? From my point of view, or my question would be, where are you tying to get back to?

CA: Back to yourself, of course.

John: (laughter) Yeah, right … hat's the whole crux. I don't believe that there is a "self."

CA: That's very interesting. Can you tell me more about that? (John and Joseph laugh)

Joseph: For this answer you need to spend a few more lifetimes. (laughter) That's one of the benefits of Walking-In-Your-Shoes, that it challenges these concepts. The Walking challenges the concept of "self."

CA: Yes, but if you're not Walking in a role, you have your own role, which could be called the "self"?

Joseph: Yes, but if you are Walking, it challenges that. It can challenge your concepts to a degree that you really have to think about your role. How realistic is it? Is it real?

CA: Yes, but is it not real? Do we not have a role in our regular lives?

John: Yes and no. We could think of us as being equipped with a "self." But if you see your self as independent or isolated from others, this notion is negative.

CA: I can understand that, John. But even if we are not independent or separate, don't we have an own role? Don't I have a role, right now? Don't you have a role, right now? Doesn't Joseph have a role, right now?

Joseph: It's interesting that you use the word "role." It's a good word for it, because we somewhat "play." We're "playing" a role.

John: Good point!

Joseph: That is real and significant; but what I also know from the Walking is that roles are shifting and changing. And the more stuck or rigid we are in a role, the harder it gets. Walking is a way of loosening that concept. I can Walk as John, or Chris, or as the trees. Is there still a Jo? Yeah, well, that's probably not going to go anywhere. But it generally comes back to …

CA: But yet nobody else can be Jo?

Joseph: That's not true. People could be Jo … (all laugh)

CA: Yes, that's right, I know what you mean. But if you were not doing it, nobody else could be Jo. If you were not here, no one else could be here as Jo.

Joseph: I hear you. I do think that there is an individual expression of life. That is unique. I'm talking about the degree to which we are attached to the uniqueness. Often, we think that's the only thing.

CA: John, what do you think? Would you dismiss any personal role or self?

John: When I die, the self is only baggage that you must discard. (laughs)

CA: Okay, that's a lot to think about for me! We should exchange texts soon. I look forward to that very much and our next meeting. See you the next time. Thank you both so much!

About the Author

In 2002, Christian Assel, who was born in 1967, graduated with an M.A.Phil in philosophy and English from the University of Hannover after many internal and external journeys, firstly in southern Europe and then throughout the world. Since 1998 he has regularly participated in seminars and workshops on Family Constellations both in Germany and overseas with luminaries such as Bert Hellinger. This was followed by a period of further training in Family Constellations with Gerhard Walper between 2003 and 2005. Since 1998 he has been active in his own right as a trainer in this field; in 2004 he first established his practice of systemic work with a "work and practice group" in Hannover, and he has since 2007 been facilitating training groups in Family Constellations. In 2005 he participated in the first North American Conference for Family Constellation work in Portland, Oregon. Since 2005 Christian Assel has regularly offered workshops in Family Constellations in San Francisco, Berlin and his home city of Hannover. In 2008 he trained in Walking-In-Your-Shoes under Joseph Culp and the same year saw the start of the first WIYS training group in Hannover.

While still at university studying philosophy Christian Assel saw clearly that his path would be less defined by theory and science than by practice and experience. The most important question for him is this: *What can we understand?* The focus of his work is not on what we imagine but what actually is and how it manifests. The effects of family ties on people's health and wellbeing play a major role in this connection. He also considers it vital to uncover and accept both the differences between people and their sameness—that is, their oneness.

For further information please go to: www.WIYS.us, see also: www.JosephCulp.com